Winning With Money

Dollars & $ense: A Comprehensive Guide to Financial Freedom & Peace

By Dan Jason

Contents

Dedication

Introduction

CHAPTER 1: Out of the Gate

CHAPTER 2: Walk Differently with Money

CHAPTER 3: Laying a Foundation: Budgeting

CHAPTER 4: Cutting Down Expenses

CHAPTER 5: More Baby Steps into the Future

CHAPTER 6: Investments 101

CHAPTER 7: Unpacking Investments Over the Long Haul

CHAPTER 8: Real Estate

CHAPTER 9: Passive Income

CHAPTER 10: Insurance Safety Nets

CHAPTER 11: Data Dive

CHAPTER 12: Baby Step 5 & Student Loans

CHAPTER 13: Living Within Your Means

CHAPTER 14: Payoff Your Home Early & Other Things that Matter

CHAPTER 15: Baby Step 7 & Financial Freedom

CHAPTER 16: Become an Everyday Millionaire

CHAPTER 17: Good Debt vs. Bad Debt

CHAPTER 18: Building a Small Business

CHAPTER 19: Creating Your Financial Blueprint

CHAPTER 20: Closing Thoughts

Acknowledgments

References

Appendix

- The Baby Step Bible (Dave Ramsey)

- Five Things that will Make you Wealthy

- Debt Snowball: How to Pay Off Debt

- Retirement Basics (Chris Hogan)

- Home Ownership & Mortgages

- 20 Tips from People Winning with Money (Dave Ramsey)

- Websites & Links

- Other Great Financial Books

- Biblical Scripture & Money

Reviews of the Author

Dedication:

This book is written for all those people out there desiring to make financial changes in their life. It is dedicated to those who might be struggling to make ends meet and to the single mom hustling to two jobs in order to provide for her kids. I wrote this for the graduate who is swimming in student loan debt, for the person who desires to save more and maximize investments, and for those who wish to take time back to retire early. Stay strong, keep working hard, and know that your discipline and desire will allow you to accumulate wealth so you can reach your dreams!

WINNING WITH MONEY $$

WINNING WITH MONEY

Dollars & $ense: A Comprehensive Guide to Financial Freedom & Peace

DAN JASON

Introduction

Money is arguably the most important resource for each of us on this planet. We use it for absolutely everything and we cannot live a single day without it. Whether we like it or not, money rules the world. The green paper that fills our wallets and the numbers in our bank accounts that paint the scope of our financial outlook, weigh heavy on us all. As an avid investor, financial enthusiast, and someone who does not want to work for the rest of my life, money matters! Each of us has inevitably faced times when money has caused great stress or even worse, detriment and panic. Hopefully you have also experienced the power in what money can afford you because being wise with capital will bring comfort, enjoyment, and hope to your world.

Finances can be one of the toughest topics for anyone to wrap their mind around. Whether you are a young kid just starting out by working your first summer job or a long time tenured businessman who knows Wall Street like the back of his hand, money still is not easy. This necessity is something we have to understand better, learn more about constantly, and utilize in new ways in order to provide for our families and to build our futures. Money has been a great source of happiness in my own life and yet it has caused great angst and heartache as well. You know how the saying goes...*Never talk about money, politics, or religion* at a dinner table. Well, if we don't start uncovering the dirty truths and expanding our personal knowledge with regard to money, we eventually won't have any left. Even worse, we won't be able to get out of debt, let alone enjoy things because that is what life is about.

Debt is something that has plagued our society for generations. However, the 21st Century has been arguably its greatest victim. We are constantly consumed by this vermin which has ransacked lives, upended relationships, and destroyed futures like nothing else. Meanwhile, there are many people who have been able to combat debt, get back to ground zero so to speak, and then build incredible wealth. Money is essential and understanding how we can take full and complete ownership over it in our lives is crucial for us all. There is no room for being naive, especially when it comes to our finances. You and I labor much too hard to continue to work and live paycheck to paycheck. It is estimated that over half of American households fly by the seat of their pants, living month to month, pinching pennies. Yes, you heard me, 50% or more of you out there are living paycheck to paycheck. This is not good and does not have to be the case. So what is happening with the other half of the population? They have it all figured out. No, not quite. Although I obviously cannot speak for everyone out there, the other half could still be doing a heck of a lot better than they are. What if I told you that by making a few simple changes in your life, your financial situation would change drastically? Would you do so? The truth is that some of you would make those adjustments in an instant, while others would blow smoke saying they would. Another group of people out there would try for a little while, before falling off the horse. Still others would resist the changes that are necessary claiming it is too hard. After all, it is your life and your money! For me it is simple. It only makes sense to maximize our dollars and cents.

After being in the workforce for over a decade, having studied finances and absorbed information like a sponge from various experts, I have found there is a much better way to live. The journey we are about to go on together will be challenging and there will be difficult changes you will have to make if you desire different results. However, I can assure you that by doing so your life will be radically altered. Not only will you see the debt disappear, the balances in those accounts continue to rise like the seas, you will provide your present self and your future self, as well as your family with amazing rewards. Nothing in life that is worthwhile and yields great dividends comes easy. You have the ability right now to take complete ownership over your finances, to educate yourself, and to take one step closer to financial freedom. Money is a beautiful thing when it isn't causing us stress and can be utilized to do what we want, when we want. Stop allowing money to control your life. Today is the day for you to take back your life and start controlling your wallet. I promise you that you will be so glad you did!

As long as you stay committed, are determined, and desire to succeed, you will. It is crucial that you do not stop. You cannot quit along the way and the setbacks you have had in the past must be learned from and set aside.

When I began understanding my own financial situation and lack of knowledge many years ago, I had to swallow a massive humility pill. Some of you out there may have to do the same. That is okay. Admitting our faults, where we went wrong or off course, and being able to quickly get back on track is key. If winning with money was easy, everyone would be doing it. I know it is human nature to get caught up in looking at what others have. We all, from time to time, have fallen susceptible to "keeping up with the Joneses" or wishing we had the life of someone who was rich. Let me tell you, the life you desire and the things you would like to have are not as far off as you might think. It is time to buckle down and to make it happen!

Throughout this book, you will find a number of personal stories that I have included from my own life, many pieces of expert level advice from the best in the world of finance, as well as data collected from research. In addition, there are short testimonies and quotations from everyday people to put our journey in perspective, and numerous strategies from those who have won in the financial realm for decades. The blend of personal narrative and financial findings along with applicable ways to approach money, will help you as the reader to formulate a winning plan that works for you. I will be as transparent as possible about my own finances because it is important for you to know that if I can do it, you can too! Keep in mind, all of the knowledge that has been compiled and everything that you read are all suggestions. They work when done and done well, but it is your money and your life so you have to own it. At the end of the day, you know what is most important to you, however I believe you will be much happier with more money to do more with. Throughout this journey together, I will outline some great methods, share with you a number of tools and resources, as well as initiate specific challenges for you to complete. These challenges are to encourage you to take the steps toward financial freedom. Although I don't know everything about money, nor will I claim so, what I do know is how I have changed my life over the past years. This has been instrumental in building personal wealth and providing a better life for my family. By the end of this book you will be more equipped with increased knowledge and a plan that if applied, will reshape your life. Now, it's go time! Let's get started. You know how the saying goes, "Time is Money!" Before we begin, I want to congratulate you on making the best investment possible, investing in yourself. There is nothing more important than taking the time to become educated to empower yourself so you can build your future. My philosophy has been and always will be, build your mind and your bank account at the same time. There is nothing wrong with that. Let the journey begin!

"Financial freedom is available to all those who learn about it and work for it."

– Robert Kiyosaki

CHAPTER 1: Out of the Gate

As a former educator for nearly a decade I understand the value of teaching and learning. Having had the opportunity to provide meaningful education to middle school students, work with high schoolers, and teach adults, there is nothing more satisfying than seeing it "click." When the lightbulb goes off in one's mind and a student has an aha moment, it is a beautiful thing. When that knowledge is applied and changes are made, nothing can top it. I desire for you to have many of these moments. What is even more however, is that I want you to not only learn about money, but to gain insights and applicable strategies to win with money. In order to do that it is critical that we set some ground rules, lay a solid foundation, and then hit the ground running.

Winning with money takes focus and discipline. I realize that is not what most people want to hear, but if you can break the mold of those habits over the first sixty or so days it will become easier as time passes and eventually you will reshape your new normal. Your mind is your most powerful weapon and tool, so it is up to you to take the right approach. For some of us, this means rewiring our brains. Turn off those channels that say, "I can't," "I don't want to," and "It is never going to happen." As the great money maker and entrepreneur Henry Ford said, "Whether you think you can or you can't, you are right." We are going to be right, and the lane we are driving in is the one going straight to the bank! So the first ground rule is a positive mindset and remaining open to trying new things, namely these strategies I will share with you. In order to win you must do some things differently. Chances are if you were already achieving all of your financial goals, you would not have picked up this book. Either way, we can all do better and must work hard to achieve what we desire. I encourage you to utilize what is offered and allow it to run its course. In due time, you will see progress. There is no magical, one shot, quick fix. The secret is, this is an ongoing process and takes time and effort on a regular basis, yet it is well worth it. With that said, the more discipline you have and the more you put your foot down on the gas pedal, the faster you will reach your financial goals.

It is important for you to realize that we are in this together. Every challenge that is laid out for you in this book is to take you to the next level. Each challenge has been designed specifically and intentionally to support you. It will provide a way for you to implement the skill or strategy that will improve your financial outlook and yield tangible results. If you stay committed and hungry, money will become your greatest ally and asset. So why take advice from a former teacher, a guy living a middle class life in the suburbs of upstate New York? Well, for starters, I live in a state that has more taxes than any place on planet earth...haha. All jokes aside, chances are if you are reading this, like me, you desire to better your situation. You don't have it all figured out and that is okay. At 31 years old I have had some great success with money. My personal portfolio continues to grow because I have utilized the strategies in this book, as well as applied the knowledge that I now want to share with you. Having paid off my house that I bought in four years for a little under $200,000, while living on a teacher's salary was a big win. Being able to build a retirement portfolio that is well into the six digit realm, and investing in stocks, bonds, and index funds has been totally transforming my financial outlook for the long run. Living a debt free life where I have the flexibility to enjoy day to day pleasures, while balancing a well diversified portfolio is something you might enjoy as well.   Or maybe you are somebody who likes to travel. I know I do. It has been amazing to take off and explore over 20 different countries and visit over 30 states with my wife and family over the past few years. I am not the braggadocios type and say all of this humbly. I have been blessed, however it took a great deal of hard work, effort, and applying winning financial strategies to overcome the debt and achieve financial peace. I am still on the hunt for complete financial independence. The thing is, that when you reshape and rewire your brain to become a financial guru so to speak, it doesn't leave you. The benefit is that there is more money to have more fun with and to enjoy greater experiences with people you love. Oh and I cannot forget, being extremely generous is something my wife and I enjoy. As a result of the financial situation we have built for our lives, I have traveled to many countries and areas of need serving on missions to give back. I share all of this personal information to help paint a picture of what my life is today and where it is going in the future because soon you will realize what changes I had to make. In the coming chapters you will see the steps that had to be taken and the struggle, sacrifice, and intentionality it would take to get to where I am now. The thing is, we must stay hungry.Remember, that the things that are hard in life are a process and don't come easy, but that is what makes the victory all the more sweeter. With money, however, you will see progress right away. Small adjustments will lead to new habits that will change the game.

The second ground rule is to have an accountability partner. This is huge! My wife is mine. You must be able to have someone that you trust that can make you toe the line when you don't want to or are having a day or a week where you aren't feeling it. Let's face it, this isn't always going to be pleasant and there are moments of this adventure that will flat out suck. However, if you have someone in your inner circle that you can rely on to help you stay on the plan and follow the program, you will get through those desert moments a little bit easier. For those of you who have kids or for others out there who have witnessed a child walking for the first time, call this image to mind. Think about that little one taking those first initial steps, baby steps. Little by little the youngster waddled a step or two before toppling over. It took the child time before they mastered the art of walking. Before long though, watch out! They are running all over God's creation and are hard to track. Well, that is what we are going to be set out to do. The third ground rule is to take baby steps. First, we will take some small baby steps together and in doing so we will gain the stamina and balance needed to take control of our finances. This will be done before we start sprinting full throttle and launch ourselves into a new realm of wealth. I hope everyone likes the sound of that! With the baby steps, it is crucial to follow through and complete each one in order before going on to the next. For over a half decade I have been reading, analyzing, utilizing, and following a number of great winners and experts in the world of money. One of those financial experts is Dave Ramsey. His winning program is called *Financial Peace University (FPU)*. I have read his books, including *The Total Money Makeover* and *Complete Guide to Money,* numerous times. In addition, I have heeded some great advice and implemented numerous strategies from his partner, Chris Hogan. Books like *Retire Inspired* and *Everyday Millionaires* have made an impact on me and my finances. I now teach the Financial Peace course to adults and am an avid listener of Dave's radio show, as well as Hogan's podcast. Over six million people have gone through FPU and are now winning with money! I highly suggest this comprehensive course which covers in depth, a number of the topics we will discuss together. Utilizing knowledge, developing a winning recipe, and applying what we learn is an essential component to this process.

The stuff works, it is tried and true, and it has helped me to reach the winner's circle at a young age.

When I was growing up I often heard my parents and grandparents refer to something called the envelope system. Now, years later, I am the one utilizing this old school way of departmentalizing and allocating money, assigning it to specific areas of my life, in order to keep my finances in tip top shape. We will get into this more, later one. I will expound upon the ideas of budgeting, which is arguably the most important strategy to becoming an expert in order to win with money. For now, let's take a deep dive into Dave Ramsey's baby steps, which he developed to help everyday people, like you and I, to accomplish great things with our money. The baby steps consist of seven incremental levels and can be likened to climbing a ladder. At the bottom when we are off the ladder we cannot ascend safely. When we grasp the ladder and climb one step at a time we are able to remain stable and then systematically reach the top. After the ascent when we have summited, we will enjoy a wonderfully filled wallet and a gorgeous financial view! The baby steps include the following:

Baby Step 1: Save $1000,
Baby Step 2: Pay off all debt
Baby Step 3: Save 3-6 months expenses for an emergency fund
Baby Step 4: Invest 15% for retirement
Baby Step 5: Save for your children's college fund
Baby Step 6: Pay off your home early
Baby Step 7: Build Wealth and give

"Give a man a fish and he will eat for a day, teach a man to fish and he will eat for a lifetime."

-Chinese Proverb

CHAPTER 2:
Walk Differently with Money

It is time for us to start walking a bit differently than we have in the past. Like a young child who is taking their first steps, we might wobble some out of the gate. That is fine. Don't worry, just stay focused and keep walking. If you fall, have the resilience to dust yourself off, get back up, and go. Like Neil Armstrong, the great astronaut, who was the first man on the moon back in 1969 with his friend, Buzz Aldrin, we too have to be courageous and take that first step. As the saying goes, "One small step for man, one giant leap for mankind." By taking these baby steps, we systematically and progressively inch our way closer to a quantum leap over a number of years. Let's now spend some time together unpacking the first couple of baby steps to understand this process and get started. It is time to go for a walk by taking those first steps toward financial peace and freedom!

BABY STEP 1: Save $1,000

The first thing for you to do to take the initial baby step, is to save $1,000. Yes, that is right, I want you to put away a grand. In order to become a winner with your money, we must all learn how to save and make this a priority. Consider this the training ground. Regardless of where you are at when reading this book, it is important to take the necessary time to work and to save this amount to complete an important first step. Two things will happen for you when you do this. First, you will have an account that has ten Benjamins in it! That will be a nice feeling and this level of success will be a rung in the ladder that we can build upon in the future for the next baby step. The second is that saving $1,000 will begin to instill the habit of setting aside money to accomplish a goal. Habits are contagious so let's utilize establishing positive habits. If we can set and achieve small scale goals, we will be able to accomplish significant advancement with the larger and more arduous ones. We sure as heck cannot tackle the mountain before traversing the smaller mole hill.

I remember back in the day when I began my financial journey and set out in taking my first baby step. I set that initial goal and that was my main focus. Having a target and feasible goal was huge. As my bank account balance climbed and each paycheck I deposited more money, I saw the numbers rise and with it my confidence grew. Once I hit that magic mark I got some wind in my sails and was really feeling good. You know what they say, the first step is always the hardest. Most people have good intentions, but intentions get you nowhere without action behind them. I need you to hit this specific dollar amount. Don't sell yourself short or sweep this step under the rug. You might have saved more than $1,000 in the past, but I want you to conquer this step now as it is an important part of the process. Almost is only acceptable with horseshoes and hand grenades. We want to blow our finances up and hit the mark every single time.

You will most likely have to make a number of small sacrifices along the way. Some of you will achieve this initial baby step within a month or two, while others might take a few months to do so. No matter how long it takes, get it done. Put this money into a savings account or money market account, as it will act as your first small emergency fund. Later on down the road, we will learn about how to build a full fledged emergency fund. This $1,000 is not to be dipped into or touched unless a flood starts coming in. What I mean by that is don't fall into temptation and go out for a wild night with your friends by taking money out of the baby step one fund. If you have the cash to do it, go ahead and do so. If you get a flat tire, have a medical bill, or some other unforeseen expense that comes your way, use the money. As my grandmother would say, "Save for a rainy day." We all know that life throws those curve balls our way and it will rain. Your $1,000 is a nice umbrella that will keep you dry as you keep pursuing financial peace along the way. When you have completed this first step, check it off the list. At this point, you should and deserve to feel great. One notch in your belt and a taste of victory. Now, you are ready to take the next step!

Developing a habit of saving is not easy, but is crucial and will be life changing. Growing up as a kid I remember vividly how my parents taught me how to save. There is a reason why to this day, I hate owing money and am so conscientious with my finances. Beginning in kindergarten, at age 5, I started to receive an allowance from my parents. Lucky me, free money! Not so fast. My brother and I had responsibilities around the house to pitch in, which taught us responsibility. Whether it was chores like cleaning our room, setting the dinner table, or doing the dishes as we got older, there were various things we were expected to do. My parents began giving us kids $0.50 in kindergarten, $1 in first grade, $2 in second grade, and a dollar additionally for every grade level from there on out as we worked up the ranks in school. This happened all the way through high school. Some of you might be able to relate to receiving an allowance. The power in saving, however, was next level for us being taught some memorable lessons. I still recall making a renowned trip to Walmart with my mom. It isn't typical to remember what in most cases would be a routine outing to "Wally World," but keep reading and you will soon see why this has been cemented into my memory bank. I had saved my weekly allowance for four weeks straight in hopes of buying that $2 red Hot Wheels matchbox car that initially caught my eye a number of trips ago. I took my little wallet with me, that had sports symbols on it, on that trip to Walmart. I was beaming with excitement. The anticipation brought a big smile to my little face. After my mom had gotten the items that were on her prepared shopping list, we took a swing down the Walmart toy aisle. I spotted that shiny red car matchbox car and thought to myself, wow that will soon be mine. I was filled with excitement grabbing it off the shelf and was about to march my way proudly to the register. My mom seized my attention and unexpectedly to my chagrin told me, "Dan, you are almost there buddy." What? What did she mean, I was almost there? I had saved for an entire month, each allowance, putting in that $0.50 into my piggy bank to get to my goal of $2 to be able to buy that car. I even had an extra penny to spare as the exact cost of the Hot Wheels car was $1.99. My heart sank when my mom then said some words that stuck me like a bolt of lightning, "You can't buy the car today, you still need a little more money to pay for tax." I did not know about tax, what five year old does? Needing an additional eight cents per dollar to tackle the tax that was tacked onto the purchase price, hit me hard. I would have to wait another week. My elated demeanor going into Walmart that day quickly turned to a sad little boy who was quite disappointed. I dragged myself to the parking lot looking like Eeyoore from Winnie the Pooh. I could use some honey to brighten my day. Although I certainly was not happy, this taught me a valuable lesson on the importance of saving and making sure you have enough in your piggy bank before you plan to make the purchase.

From the very beginning, this important lesson was planted in my mind. If there were things you wanted in life, you had to save up for them and then you could get them. A week later we would go back to Walmart and I would buy that shiny red Hot Wheels matchbox car. I wish I could tell you that I still had the original one today. However, that matchbox car planted within me a valuable life lesson and still serves as a symbol that I hold onto, as a prime example of the power of saving and being financially responsible. I learned from a young age that there are no handouts in life. Every time we went somewhere and I wanted to get something, I would have to be prepared and bring my own money if I wanted to make a purchase. You might be thinking, wow that is harsh for a little kid. What kind of parents do that? Don't worry or get me wrong, my parents provided all of the necessities and more. What they desired to do, they did and it stuck for the rest of my life. It was all about teaching us boys to understand the valuable and importance of money and saving. It can be likened to one of my all time favorite quotes found in Proverbs 22:6-7 which says, "Train a child in the way he should go, and when he is old he will not turn from it. The rich rule over the poor, and the borrower is servant to the lender." I plan to lay a solid foundation for my own kids someday and to teach them valuable lessons, many of which are outlined in this book. The similar winning tactics that were passed on to me, will be the ones that help establish a habit that becomes second nature from the start. This is an advantage that cannot be overlooked as the value is extreme!

CHALLENGE 1: *Save a grand by putting away $1000!*

Open a new savings account, begin a money market account, or take a large jar that you can hide somewhere in your house and start socking money away. Every time you are paid, put some more money in there. Count it each week and see how much closer you are to achieving your goal. For the ambitious crowd and financially savvy people out there, take this challenge to the next level by setting a SMART goal (we will discuss these later on) and a date or goal for yourself for when you will save up the money by. Compete against yourself or have a friendly competition with a friend. Take on an extra overtime shift, turn down that meal out, and put the money you want to spend toward your baby!! Baby step one only is achieved by getting it done. Yeah, you heard me, keep stacking that cash up and feel good when you do it. You got this!

Baby Step 2: Pay Off All Debt (Except the House) Using Debt Snowball

"When you don't have debt, your money can do anything you want it to."
-Anonymous

The four letter word that makes people cringe and must become your arch enemy is debt. Your greatest ally and asset is that other four letter word, cash. Debt is the kryptonite of cash. Learn to hate it. Despise debt at all costs and do anything and everything to slay this beast. Later on in the book we will discuss how leveraging debt can actually be a good thing and work in your favor when it comes to investing in real estate with tax breaks and accumulating wealth through passive income. As for you and I, right now, debt is public enemy number one and you have the sword in your hand, ready for battle. Personally, initiating the debt snowball is the hardest and most challenging task in my opinion. I say this because it takes great humility and honesty to get started. The reason why tens of millions of people continue to live paycheck to paycheck and could not cover a $1,000 expense that came up is because of debt. Debt is dumb. It enslaves us and makes us unable to do so many things, including having peace in our lives due to stress coming from financial instability. Being in the red is no bueno. Remember, we want that green and we want to be adding to our accounts, not draining them.

Years ago, I woke up and like most mornings made my way into the bathroom. As I got ready for the day, I looked into the mirror. This time though I spent an extra minute or two and really looked myself in the eyes. Today was the day that things were truly going to change. Saving $1,000 was a good start. I had some mountains to move and it felt like I was going to be climbing Everest. As much as I despised the situation I was in, it was the reality of my life and I could not run from it or hide. I had to initiate the debt snowball or the avalanche coming down that mountain would soon bury me for good. Baby step two is your moment of truth. It is time for you to be accountable and take a long hard look at yourself in the mirror. What do you want your future to look like? Do you want to continue to be up to your eyeballs in debt, sinking further and further into a dark hole of despair. This does not have to be your story. You can change your life and today can be the day. As I walked out of that bathroom I gained a swagger. I had a renewed pep in my step. I began to believe that I was going to crush debt and make it my… You fill in the blank, I'm trying to keep it PG over here.

Confidence is huge when it comes to our finances and in order to tackle baby step numero dos, I had to build mine. So what is the debt snowball anyway? This part of baby step two is where we tackle debt. I liken it to being a football player at the opposite goal line. You are the running back and the quarterback is ready to snap the ball. He will soon hand it off to you. There is 100 yards in front of you and every step forward you make, you are running down debt. There is one problem, seeing nothing but green turf in your field of vision is not the case. The route to the opposite end zone has many hurdles to jump over, obstacles to maneuver around, and opponents to bust through. All of this is, in short, debt. The linebackers and massive defensive tackles are running at you at full steam and trying to drag you backward. You persist and give one a stiff arm, juke another, and a third steam roll. You continue to chip away picking up first down after first down, marching your way down the field. Like a great running back you persist and continue to ground and pound. At last, you have high stepped your way into the end zone and scored that touchdown to even the score! Debt has been erased, it is a new ball game and you are set up to win the game!

The first thing that you have to do in baby step two in order to set off on your debt free journey is to list out all of your debts from smallest to greatest. After doing so, you put any extra money at the end of the month that you have left over, after all of your essentials are paid, toward that first and smallest debt. It is important for us to take a brief moment to discuss essentials. Back in elementary school we learned the difference between wants and needs. What I mean by this term, essentials or needs, is your four walls (housing), food, electricity/heat (utilities), and clothing. More on the big four in a little bit. Outside of that, everything else is technically an unessential, or a want. Sorry, but not really. You are after all working toward slaying debt. The debt snowball has been set in motion as you continue to chip away at that first debt. It might be a balance on a credit card, a small personal loan, or some other expense that you owe. Pay it off in full, and do so as quickly as possible. Then, move on to the next one. For you advanced financial readers out there, you might be saying, why wouldn't I tackle the debt that has the highest interest rate first? If you are one of those people with that question, the good news is that you have some knowledge that will be tapped into later on down the road. This is a great idea and approach as long as the debt you are facing and paying off is not so big that it is an immovable mountain. What we don't want is to halt progress and then give up on this all together. That would be detrimental. Chipping away little by little by tackling the smallest debt first, allows us to gain progress. By seeing results, we build confidence, and are able to start taking ownership over our lives. If all of your debts are around the same dollar amount, within a few thousand dollars, then you might want to prioritize them by attacking the one that has the highest interest rate first. This strategy will allow you to save yourself more money in the long run. You then keep the pads and helmet on and repeat the process until you reach the end and pay off your last or final debt. For most of you out there, getting to ground zero (debt free) and evening the score, will be the most difficult and lengthy task. However, it can and will get done, but you have to do it. There is no other secret formula or magic potion. Nothing besides hard work, saving, and determination can make debt go away. There might be one obstacle between you and the goal line, or perhaps there are many. The important thing is that you start running. Pick up traction and shed debt like the great running back, Walter Peyton, shed defenders on his way to the end zone.

There are some things that you can do specifically to help speed up the debt snowball process. As many financial gurus say, "Your income is your greatest wealth building tool." This is so true. So should you go and quit your job to find a new one because you don't make enough money and are still in debt? No!! Instead, pick up another side hustle, a second job, a part time gig, or establish another way to make money outside of your 9-5. This might mean waiting tables on the weekend or evenings, utilizing your talents in a new way to make some money, picking up some extra shifts at work when they are available, or doing all the above. Get creative. Everyone has the same amount of time in a day. If you have the typical work schedule, you work on average, 40 hours a week. There are another 128 hours out there in the course of your week ready to be utilized. Make the most of them and debt will decrease. Sacrifice during this stage of the game is imperative. As Dave

Ramsey says often on his radio show, "You shouldn't see the inside of a restaurant unless you work in one." No, your life is not over, well maybe for a little while. However, what you have to do is to cut down your expenses as much as possible and increase your income as high as it can go during this stage of the process. Think of it as a symbiotic relationship. Like two animals that help one another out in the wild, the one benefits the other and in return, the first helps out the second. If you do both simultaneously, by increasing your income and chopping down expenses, you will slay the dragon and triumph over debt.

Personally, I have paid off over $170,000 in debt. Yes, you read that amount correctly. Some of you are probably thinking, yikes, I should jump ship on this crazy author now. I tell you this so you can understand where I came from and how I got to where I am today. Soon I will be eclipsing the half million dollar mark of total net worth. I have my eyes set on that cool million down the road because I understand how it will change the game for my family and those around me. It is only a matter of time for you to get there as well, but you have to hammer away at that debt. Credit cards, personal loans, interest payments, a mortgage, car debt, and Sallie Mae all had to be slain in my household to become debt free. I would be remiss to say that this was easy. It was certainly not. My wife would probably say it was the hardest thing we have ever done together. Yet, it is just that, it is done! Never will we put ourselves in that daunting situation again. See, once you get back to ground zero and even the score, that is when you start building real wealth and money becomes your greatest ally.

In order to pay down that debt and not allow it to consume us, my wife and I created a strict budget and game plan. This served as the blueprint for our lives over the next few years so we could become debt free. Damn, he didn't just say months, he said years. I know that is what you might be thinking. Keep in mind a couple years is far better than an entire lifetime. Well, there were celebratory moments along the way when we reached milestones to help keep us going. Unlike some financial activists out there, I personally believe that it is important to reward yourself a little bit when you achieve your goals. Otherwise, most people will eventually quit altogether. The average person cannot go full throttle every day, all day. If you are one of those people, that is awesome. Personally I am naturally an all in type of guy who can push the pedal to the metal and have that gazelle like intensity. My wife on the other hand, is not. It doesn't come naturally to her to do so. However, remaining focused and intentional is crucial. Being able to see the next goal you set for the debt payoff and visualizing it by using charts where you color in your progress or some other metric can be helpful. The biggest and most important thing that I want to stress about baby step two and the debt free journey however, is that it's a marathon, not a sprint! I hope you come out of the gate running fast and furious, but don't burn yourself out too quickly. In order to stay well balanced and be able to conquer debt, as well as set yourself up for future success, budgeting is a must. So let's work together and get that budget party started!

"A budget is telling your money where to go instead of wondering where it went."

-Dave Ramsey

CHAPTER 3: Laying a Firm Foundation

BUDGETING

Another word in the English language that makes people run for the hills or want to go and hide from is the word, budget. Smart people and wealthy people live by it, broke and stupid people ignore it. Blunt, yes, but also very true. The six letter word kicked me in the mouth hard. I might as well have taken a bite out of the damn curb. A wave of oh shoot, that is what I have to do pounded me like a tsunami. I am not going to lie, budgeting is not easy. However, budgeting is a must as it will allow you to utilize every single dollar you make. This one financial strategy that has been around for centuries, yet followed very inconsistently, will be what helps pay off debt. Your budget will maximize your money for the goals and dreams you have in the years to come. It is about time that we tell our money where to go and that is what your budget will do.

When I was in college, as many students were racking up student loan debt, I opened my first credit card. Then I added another, and yet another. The evil pieces of plastic in my wallet became addicting. Most days I had more cards in my pocket than dollar bills, talk about a problem. Many of you are probably thinking, this guy really is crazy, who doesn't have two, three, or even four credit cards. Just think of the rewards points you can earn and the fact that it's impossible to carry all that cash around all the time. Cut them up! If you want to destroy debt and utilize a winning budget, get out a pair of scissors right now and cut those thieves up once and for all! I am dead serious. You can't spend money you don't have if you want to win and make money for your future. I wish I would have taken my own advice years ago, but I did not know any better. Or at least that is what I told myself before I became fully accountable with my finances. What a load of crap, that is just another excuse. Principle number three to abide by, stop making excuses. They get you nowhere. Stop throwing yourself a pity party and man up. We got work to do people! I know it might be a struggle and you will give a number of reasons to explain why you need every one of those credit cards that hamper your progress and have for a ton of Americans been their key to debt. The question remains, how badly do you want this? If you can do what is really hard, you will prove to yourself that slaying debt really matters. If not, your wishy washy non committed self may indeed fall back into bad habits and the snowball of debt will steam roll you on it's way back down the mountain. You can always take out a credit card down the line when you are debt free and have taken complete ownership of your finances. Now, it is time to cut ties, after all, we can't swipe what we don't have.

As I racked up the credit card debt, and saw money enter my bank account and leave so quickly like it was never there, I got frustrated. How could I have a decent teaching job right out of college and yet no money to show for it. After looking at my credit card statements and what I was spending money on, I began to realize that there were so many things I didn't need that I was just throwing my money away on. It was almost as if I took sets of twenty dollar bills, crumpled them up and threw them in the trash can. Who does that? Eating out numerous days a week, but that was what bachelor's do, I told myself. Getting the newest Jordan sneakers for my collection, but I wanted them. I deserved those fresh kicks. Half the time I didn't even realize what I was spending my money on until it was far too late. That was when I decided, today is the day that I am going to begin tracking my expenses. What I would find out by doing this would be alarming, but there is only one way to beat the bully and that is to fight him! It was time to punch back. Tracking expenditures is the first step toward building a budget.

Truth be told, the word budget should not scare you. It is going to become your friend. A budget is simply a written plan that tells your money where to go each month. This tool will be instrumental in helping you win. Before you know where to put your money or how much of it needs to go toward various expenditures and avenues in your life, you need to do a comprehensive analysis of your financial expenses. What the heck is he talking about? To simplify it, over the next three months I want you to do what I did, track everything you spend money one. I have my students and clients who I guide with their money log it all. I mean chart everything. Whether it is a typical expense that covers the essentials, like your rent or mortgage payment, or it is a $0.30 toll, write it down. Below you will find a comprehensive financial analysis tracker for you to use so that you can begin recording your expenditures. I suggest that you use and create this sheet. Customize it to fit what you spend money on and keep it in your phone in the notes section so you have it with you at all times. The subject lines that I created are based on common expenses and things the average person might spend money on during a month to month basis. However, feel free to change those based on your lifestyle.

Two things will happen when you do this and take the first serious step toward building a budget. Firstly, it will give you a clear idea of where your money is going. For me, this made me furious. How can getting angry be a good thing? Well, it ignited a burning passion in me to not allow money to control my life. Instead, I was going to take my life back and totally control my hard earned money by making it go where I wanted it to go! Secondly, using the comprehensive financial analysis expenditures resource, aka the tracking of your expenses, will hold yourself accountable. It is much more difficult to spend money on useless things when you have to write it down and stare it in the face every day. Think back to when you were in full pads at the opposite goal line, ready to square off against your debt. You had to be fearless and look that enemy in the eyes. Then it was time to start running up hill, building endurance along the way. You might think that this seems ridiculous or even anal to jot down even meagre dollar gum purchases or the $5 coffee from Starbucks that you enjoy. You will be very surprised to see how it all adds up and contributes to the scope of your life and your bank account. And if you are anything like me, or how I was at the time, it will show you why you have a red number in your bank account which is a tough pill to swallow. The last thing to say before you take a look at the tracking tool below which I developed for you to use, is that doing this for three straight months is necessary. The reason why is because then you will take the average to get a more clear indication of your expenses. There are always things that don't happen on the regular, outliers per say that show up from time to time. Taking account over a three month period will help us to gain a more accurate picture of the actual financial situation we are in. During career changes, a move to a new area, or times when your income has been altered significantly for better or worse, I suggest re-aligning your budget by doing another three or so month assessment to map it out. I am willing to bet that for most of you out there who are really taking this thing seriously, month two will have less expenses recorded than month one, and month three even less than month two. Somehow your competitive nature will be tapped into, it just happens that way when we are intentional about our spending. Below you will find the tracker which I left blank for your use. Again, I encourage you to take this tool and plug it into your phone to have it wherever you go.

Financial Expenditures Analysis Sheet
Month:
Net income per month:
Total Household income per month:$

Mortgage/rent:$
Home owners/rent insurance: $
Student loans: $
Health Insurance:
Life Insurance: $
Credit card payment (debt): $
Car payment/lease: $
Car care: $0
Car Insurance: paid
Gas: $
AAA membership: $
Groceries: $
nutrition/vitamins: $
Cell Phone: $
NAT GRID (heat & electric):$
Trash Service: $
Water Bill:
Natural Yard Waste Collection:
Church Giving: $
Other giving/charities: $
Gym membership: $
TV: $
Internet: $
Security System: $
Clothing: $
Cleaning/laundry: $
Toiletries: $
Cosmetics:

Gifts (Birthdays/Christmas, etc): $
Weddings: $0
Entertainment/fun money: $
Vacation: $
Dan Portland Trip: $
Allowance: $
Miscellaneous expenses: $
EZ pass & tolls: $
Bills & spending money: $

THIS MONTH Actual Expenses:
Monthly Grand Total:$

$_____ *Left after all bills paid*
Put the extra toward Baby Step 1 or Baby Step 2 (Debt Snowball) depending on where you are at in the process. If you don't have debt and have $1,000 saved...stow it away in a savings account for now.

Money Saved after all expenses paid: $_____

When using this tracking resource, repeat this process over the next three months and then take each category and do an overall inventory. Decide if the expenses in a given section is a necessity. There are some things that you can cut down to chop off expenses, but again it will take sacrifice. For me it was things like cutting off the cable TV and subscribing to a low cost streaming service. I put myself on a spending freeze for quite some time. I literally set a timer which counted up in my phone and I tried to go as long as possible without spending a single penny. For me, this meant no more trips to the mall to get the latest Jordan sneakers. Dinners out went bye bye! And well, there was that bar bill that accumulated like a nor'easter snow storm hitting in the middle of winter, that had to go too. So that meant buying some beer and inviting friends over instead of going out. After you see the three months unfold, you will identify patterns. You will also recognize clear areas where you can cut down the spending or completely extinguish it altogether. Think of this exercise as attacking the enemy. In order to win in a sporting event or war, it is crucial to understand our areas of weakness and to shield ourselves from attack. Meanwhile, it is ever so critical to stay on the aggressive side and conquer by going after the enemy. Remember, when doing your inventory, those essentials must stay and then everything else is a matter of choice. The more you sacrifice and trim down the wants, the quicker your debt will be paid off and you will reach your next set of goals. If you desire to keep all of the creature comforts and make no adjustments, it is going to extend the length of time you will endure this program significantly. At the end of the day it is up to you to decide, but I hope you will find motivation to make changes happen after seeing where your money went over those months. This is the first step toward building your budget and establishing new habits when it comes to spending the money you work hard for on the regular.

Building Your Budget

Now that you have done the financial assessment and analysis from the past three months of expenditure charting, you are ready to build a solid budget. Hopefully you have prioritized things by now and have separated needs from wants. The less item lines in your budget the better, as this means you will be spending fewer amounts of money on a monthly basis. In return, this will afford you a greater opportunity to put any extra cash toward your debt snowball and for future investments down the road. To begin, take the four essentials: housing, food, clothing, and electricity/heat (utilities), those go at the top of the budget. Plug in the numbers for those line items. Next, jot down for your other categories such as transportation, health insurance, cell phone, etc. and keep working your way down the budget line. You should know at this point how much money you brought in over the past three months and have divided that by three to get the average for what you are working with in terms of income. This is your total pot of disposable income or cash. Remember, that this is your greatest wealth building tool and factor in the equation. If you have decided to pick up some extra shifts, a second job, or part time gig, great! This will add to the overall total pot of money you have to draw from and will increase your power with your budget. However, even if you have a second job or are taking on overtime work, this should go at the top of your budget in the overall total household income section. As Dave Ramsey suggests, you should try your best to do what he calls the "every dollar budget." What this means is that you literally assign every dollar that you make and take home to the categories in your itemized budget sheet for the month. Anything that is left over, once all of the essentials and bills are accounted for, goes straight toward your debt snowball. For those of you out there who might not have any debt, you will begin fully funding your emergency fund, which is going to be the next topic of discussion in the following chapter.

Once this budget is built it should serve as your blueprint or game plan to win during this next month. It is critical that you stick to the plan. If you decide to deviate or not follow the plan, the words on the paper itself are not going to be of any use. Too many times when I have mentored people and advised them with their finances, they had this amazing plan they worked really hard on, but it was for naught. The individual or couple started the month out strong, but then stepped off the path to success. They stopped following their budget. Do not allow this to be you. I realize this may be new to you and it can even feel constraining. Believe me, my wife hated the "B" word, she despised our budget when we began. However, like her, I hope that you will soon realize that by assigning every dollar and telling your money where to go, you will see great results and there will be more cash to work with to help you get to the next step or stage in the game. Well, Dan, this budget thing is something I only have to do for a little while right? I mean once I am out of debt and even the score at zero again, we can drop the budget and start living large! Not quite.

Did you know that the average millionaire in America, over 95% of them, continue to still live on a budget. You are probably wondering why? If you had a million dollars in the bank or invested, a budget would be the last thing on your mind. Well, that might be the very reason why you don't have that kind of net worth or stacks of cash to draw on! A winning formula that works whether you take in $2,000 a month or $10,000 every four weeks is the budget. The good news is that you will grow accustomed to this and before you know it, budgeting will become second nature. Your accountability partner will be huge with this baby step also. Even if that person is not someone that you live with or have joint accounts attached to, it is a great idea to share budgeting notes and progress. This will ensure that you stay on track. After all, when I began there were many moments when I was about to buy something I clearly did not need. The thing that stopped me was the fact that I didn't want to have to admit a stupid or impulsive purchase to my accountability partner the next time that we spoke.

Lastly, when it comes to budgeting, this plan can and will have to be flexible as time continues. What I mean by that is that at points the numbers will have to change due to an array of factors. Some of which we control, while others we do not. For example, rent and insurances often increase over time, usually year to year. Therefore, some more money will have to be factored in when those variables are on the rise. If you have another child or your high schooler goes off to college, this will impact line items in your monthly budget, especially when it comes to food, utilities, and more. Not to mention, if you are helping them navigate through college, tuition and room/board will increase your budget expenses significantly. Regardless of your current situation, things will inevitably change in the future. Hopefully in a more positive direction. It is okay when adjustments need to be made. Don't panic, just adjust. My main desire is that you continue to work hard and do all you can to cut down those purchases, meanwhile increasing your disposable income through making more money. By conducting your monthly budget and allocating money wisely by assigning it to each budget line item, you will win in this area. That is why my parents and grandparents used the old school envelope system. Remember, at this point hopefully you took my advice and cut up those credit cards. You can keep a debit card so that automatic payments of bills can be withdrawn for the essentials monthly, but that other plastic should be long gone and at the bottom of the garbage heap! Utilize cash and create different envelopes for each itemized subject line in your monthly budget. Go to the bank and take out the physical money for each and put it in the envelopes so it can be paid out on time and used throughout the month. This is crazy! No still actually does that do they? I know what you might be thinking. Trust me, try it. It works. Not to mention, what do you have to lose by doing something new? How I figure is if the way I was doing things hasn't been working the best, it is time to do something new. The definition of insanity is, doing the same thing over and over and expecting different results. No, I am not calling you insane, but I was there once too. My wheels were spinning and I was going nowhere. That is no way to live. For the automatic payments you set up to be withdrawn from your checking account, just put a sticky note with the amount on it for the rent, or cell phone bill for example in the envelope. As for the other expense categories, put in each envelope the cold hard cash. This will do. If the money runs out in your food budget category, make due with what you have. See, the thing is, that people statistically spend 15% less when they carry around cash to spend than when they pay with a card. There is a connection that happens in our brains and it has an affect on us when we have to reach into the wallet. Digging out the green and paying on the spot helps put a governor on our spending.

I am excited for you, as budgeting is going to transform your life from the get go. You can do this. Don't worry about your neighbors or your friends. And yes, some people might even think or call you weird. I am okay with that because in order to get different results you have to live and do things differently. Trust me, you will be feeling great when you have extra money laying around after the essentials are paid for and all your bills are settled before the due date. When you can call up the credit card company and put $200 or $300 extra toward that debt or you are able to chip away at those student loans by making an extra $100 payment, you are rewarding your future self. Being disciplined isn't enjoyable and is certainly not easy. As Hebrews 12:11 states, "No discipline seems pleasant at the time, but painful. Later on, however, it produces a harvest of righteousness and peace for those who have been trained by it." Implementing your budget and paying off your debt in baby step two are a couple more ways for you to gain some more notches in your belt as you keep marching towards financial freedom.

CHALLENGE #2: Track ALL of your EXPENSES over the next 3 months & rebuild your budget.

Whether you are new to this budgeting process or have had a budget for many years, I want you to commit toward completing this challenge. For those of you out there who are familiar with the budgeting process and have been following a strict one for years, still record all of your expenses over the next few months and follow the plan as prescribed in this chapter. It will help you reallocate money and reassess what is necessary and essential versus what can be expelled or at least trimmed down. Below I have included the budget sheet for you to use. Again, I highly encourage you to implement the envelope system. Using these strategies will definitely help you pack a serious punch and you may be pleasantly surprised, like I was. My hope is that in a matter of a couple months, you will see that there is actually a lot more money available when I tell it where to go. Money is great, especially when we are good stewards and are in control of our spending.

MONTHLY BUDGET SHEET
Month:
Total Household income:$
Mortgage/rent:$
Home owners/rent insurance: $
Student loans: $
Health Insurance: $
Life Insurance: $
Car payment/lease: $

Car care: $0
Car Insurance: paid
Gas: $
AAA membership: $
Groceries: $
nutrition/vitamins: $
Cell Phone: $
NAT GRID (heat & electric/utilities):$
Trash Service: $
Water Bill:
Natural Yard Waste Collection:
Church Giving: $
Other giving/charities: $
Gym membership: $
TV: $
Internet: $
Security System: $
Clothing: $
Cleaning/laundry: $
Toiletries: $
Cosmetics:
Gifts (Birthdays/Christmas, etc): $
Weddings: $0
Entertainment/fun money: $
Vacation: $
Dan Portland Trip: $
Allowance: $
Miscellaneous expenses: $
EZ pass & tolls: $
Bills & spending money: $

THIS MONTH Actual Expenses:
Monthly Grand Total:$

$_____ Left after all bills paid

Baby Step #1 ($1000 goal) fund: $
Credit card payment (debt payoff): $
Extra Student loan (debt payoff): $
Extra Car loan (debt payoff): $
Other debt pay off: $

Total Snowball Debt Pay off this month: $

Money Saved after all expenses paid: $ 0

*Note, this bottom line should be $0. This is because you are using the Dave Ramsey *Every Dollar Budget* approach where you assign literally every dollar you make to a category and have nothing left at the end of the month. Any extra money, after your items in your budget were accounted for, should be thrown 100% at debt. If you don't have any debt, start saving it up. As you build your savings, you will get a head start toward your full emergency fund, which is notably baby step 3.

"The habit of saving is itself an education; it fosters every virtue, teaches self-denial, cultivates the sense of order, trains to forethought, and so broadens the mind."

– T.T. Munger

CHAPTER 4: Cutting Down Expenses

"Give me six hours to chop down a tree and I will spend the first four sharpening the axe." -Abraham Lincoln

So far we have spent ample time on two very important baby steps in the journey to financial freedom and peace. Conjointly, we have discussed my favorite and an extremely applicable tool, the budget. My hope is that this new information is being absorbed and is exciting you. Keep in mind, your budget in no way is to limit your life, but in essence, it is what will give you more opportunity to have a more fruitful one. A decreased amount of stress occurs when we know where all of our money is going during the course of a given month, as well as freeing up extra cash which becomes available to hit our target goals. I am confident that you are going to win with this new blueprint that you have created and are now following as a road map for your success with money. However, there are many more things to cover in later chapters that will help you drastically when it comes to how to make money on the money you already have. It energizes me to think of the many ways we will be able to grow our accounts by maximizing the money we bring in each month. I am very excited to share those with you soon, but we are not there yet.

It is critical for us to take some time to brainstorm and lay out some tangible ways for the average person to cut down their expenses on a monthly basis. Like Abe Lincoln indicated to open our chapter, we don't want to be swinging some ordinary old axe. Let's work to sharpen it so each swing can slice our expenses sharply. After being a financial advisor and teaching FPU classes to many people over the years, ways to lower and eventually minimize expenses must not and cannot be brushed over. I would be doing you all a severe disservice if that were the approach. Some of the tactics and suggestions we will discuss in this section, you might already be doing. If that is the case, keep on keeping on! There will be a number of others that will seem like, duh I should have thought of that, and still others that you hadn't even heard of before. The main goal and thing to focus on is how we can cut down those expenses, meanwhile still taking care of the essentials and not live like a pauper.

Discipline with our finances is a key theme of this book. Allow it to sink in if it has not already. Think of it like that new hit single you hear on repeat. You will be listening to this word spoken often and eventually it will be like the air you breathe, as it is a necessity to win with money! Your initial response to many of these tactics and strategies, options, and ways of doing things differently may be similar to my wife's. "Ah, I don't want to do this!" or "Do we have to?" And then there is my favorite one of them all, "This is ridiculous and so annoying!" It is okay if you react in this manner and frankly I don't even care. I say this because I care about you and your future. If you even implement one of these strategies or tips, you can cut down your expenses and have more money for that debt snowball, savings, or investing which we will cover down the line. Cutting down your monthly and annual expenses for that matter is my main and only objective here. So if you hate me for this or not, I can live with it. I am fine with being disliked, after all, discipline is typically not anyone's best friend. Well, unless you are me that is!

Right off the bat, I want you to examine your budget line items. Take another close look. At this point you should be very familiar with them. Although I don't expect you to know them like the back of your hand, they are no longer like an alien invasion. The once foreign and unknown expenses are quite recognizable. There are some big ticket items in the essentials category and there are some mid and small range expenses. Meanwhile, there are other non essentials that we can still cut out altogether. So what we will do is first focus on the non essentials and then take on the necessary big four. This plan of attack will help you formulate a way to trim down the "have to pay" items, which will remain fairly constant over the long haul. Now is the time to implement the minimalist mentality and live out that lifestyle at least for a little while.

Television

According to a report from *Decision Data* that was completed in March of 2020, American households on average were paying upwards of $217.42 per month for their cable package. So if you are sitting there feeling good about yourself because your Spectrum Cable or Verizon Fios bill came in at $150 for this past month, don't be! Yeah, you heard me, CUT THE CORD! It is interesting, scissors are becoming one of your best friends! Haha. May I remind you about the last time we used those on the credit cards! Well, that is exactly what I decided to do numerous years ago, the cable had to go. So Dan, you mean no more entertainment for me to watch at night after a long stressful day at work? Nope. You will now be reading, playing board games, or watching paint dry. I'm just kidding. None of that at all, well of course you are always welcome to an entertainment you desire. That is of course as long as it doesn't involve cable, a dish or some high cost network. At this point there are so many options out there for streaming services, it is silly not to utilize at least one of them. I have tried and used a number of these (not all at once of course) over the past several years. Sling TV, YouTube TV, Spectrum Streaming, the list goes on. Most of you probably already have a Netflix account or are tapping into a friend's anyway. So when you pair your Netflix or Hulu subscription with one of these other streaming services you will probably come in at around a total of less than $35 per month! Just by cutting the cord and making this change, you just freed up somewhere between $125 to $150 or more by making a single switch. I bet you won't even miss the extra 100 or more channels that you never watched anyway. The best part is that most streaming services allow you to pick the channels you desire. And for my audience out there who is ultra hard core, you can buy an HD antenna for about $20, connect it to your TV and pick up the local channels for free. That along with you Netflix account or just utilizing what the antenna picks up can give you free TV. Besides, books are better for your brain anyway, but you already knew that since you are reading this one!

Cell Phones

The second big ticket item that sucks the life out of people's pockets and robs their wallets on a monthly basis is the cell phone plan. Before you close this book on me and try to return it from where you purchased it, hear me out. Like you, we cannot live in the 21st Century without a cell phone. It is impossible. I by no means am asking you to even consider that. Nor am I asking you to go back to the so called dark ages during a time when the phone booth existed. Possibly you are old enough to have heard of the day when there was only one telephone land line for an entire neighborhood. My grandparents have told me stories of when they would pick up the phone and could listen in on a conversation between two people, having to wait to use the phone for their own call. Don't worry, I am not requiring you to go back into the past. If I did, I would truly be crazy! However, there are many great options out there for a fraction of the cost that I fully believe will give you the same high quality service, yet cut your bill in possibly more than half.

According to J.D. Power & Associates, way back in 2009, well over ten years ago, 46% of Americans said that their monthly cell phone bill was over $100 per month. 13% had a bill back then that topped $200! In 2020, reports estimate that the average individual's cell phone bill is nearly $120 per month! That is crazy! Even though it hasn't gone up that much over a decade, the concept of a cell phone to do the basics is practically obsolete. Data has taken us to the next level. I understand that our phones are now handheld computers. Believe me, I have an iPhone too! My iPhone 8 is a huge upgrade from my iPhone 4 which lasted for literally 11 years. What? They are expensive and my mentality is, it isn't broken, don't fix it. Oh, and sorry Droid fans out there I am an Apple guy. However, the need to have a cellular device is not an excuse to get sucked into the dark hole and vortex of an industry that keeps reaching into our pockets and taking our money! If you are past baby step 3 and are investing, you might want to consider tapping into the billions of dollars that are out there in the realm of cloud computing, technology, and cellular companies! There is a better and cheaper way people. I have invested my money in this sector, it's a win win. By doing my research and finding a better avenue, I went from paying $85 a month with my AT&T contract plan to $31/month. How can that be? Well, instead of paying by contract, I switched to pay as you go and that saved me over $50 per month right off the rip. For those of you who are big time data users, you can still have a phone plan with companies like Sprint for $45/month that includes unlimited talk, text, and data. Do your homework and cut down this huge expense. Just think, wouldn't you prefer to spend $372 annually as opposed to $1,500. That's over $1,100 in savings for a single year. Put that money in some good growth stock mutual funds or an index fund and let it accumulate for the next 30 years and you will have upwards of $150,000. Mind blowing I know! And that is from a single change in a cell phone plan. Combine that with cutting your cable bill and you could see $300,000 more in your net worth over the next few decades. I might be onto something! As you can see I am pretty amped up about this and will have lots to share in the coming chapters.

Transportation

The third big expense that you can cut down on is transportation, this might be the biggest of them all outside of the big four. Don't worry, I have a car. Although, it would be nice to be able to walk or bike everywhere. For those of you who live in a big metropolitan area and can take public transit, fantastic. That is a great way to travel and more affordable to boot. Whether you do own a vehicle or not, this section is worth the read as I will get into crunching some numbers that will surely blow you away. Chances are, someday in the future, you will purchase or have a vehicle in your household.   When that time comes and you do, it is important to make some fiscally sound decisions. Based on reports run by lendingtree.com in 2020, the average monthly car payment in the U.S. was $550 for new vehicles, $393 for used cars and $452 for vehicles that were leased. Overall, Americans collectively owe more than $1.2 trillion in auto loan debt and debt from vehicles makes up about 9.5% of all American consumer debt! That is wild! Go back to your budget right now and take a quick look at your monthly car payment. This might be another moment of truth for you. If you are under the amounts that are reported above, that is a good thing, but you are not out of the woods yet! What if I told you that you could realistically cut your car payment in half or possibly not have a monthly payment at all. Let's start with cutting down the payment.

Look at what is in your driveway or parked on the street corner. This is your vehicle, something you depend on to drive you to work each day, and it is used to get your family safely from place to place. Like you, I also rely on my car. However, why spend so much on something we sit in for so little time every day, in order to try to impress people we don't even know at a stop light? According to a recent report from the *New York Post*, Americans on average spend about 35-40 minutes per day commuting. The longest commute time is out west in cities like Los Angeles or places that are spread far apart. In states where people commute into cities from the far off country or suburbs, time behind the wheel is increased, but even that is about an hour on average daily. A general rule of thumb in order to be financially responsible when it comes to your vehicle is to not spend more than 10% of your gross monthly pay (before tax income) on your car payment. So for you who like to roll big and deep with those top of the line head jerking vehicles, it might be time to reconsider. Yeah, I am talking about you drivers of those Beamers, Benzes, Bentleys, and big trucks. Today might be the day to think about some things about your vehicle. If you have a net worth of over a million dollars, enjoy the ride! We can always upgrade in the car department when our finances are in line and the debt has been kicked to the curb. For most of us, the reassessment of our vehicle situation has indeed begun. If you are more practical or you really want to win with money over the long haul, get behind the wheel of something less expensive now and then later on down the road (pun fully intended) you can ride in that swagger wagon! A low budget car payment like a Honda Civic, Toyota Corolla, or even a mid size SUV can be super affordable. Why not try to spend $150-$200 per month, much more affordable. Saving that extra $200-$300 a month will pump serious cash into your bank account. Just think, how would you feel knowing you had another $3,600 per year to work with. Not to mention you will save on car insurance, maintenance, and money at the pump! The increased money acquired from the vehicle swap could be used to take that dream vacation, enjoy fun experiences with family and friends, or be invested.   Just think, over the next 25 years your choice to drive more humbly could turn into another $300,000! You are catching on quick and are on your way to becoming debt free in no time. If you keep walking in this direction, becoming that everyday millionaire will happen much sooner than you thought! My favorite option of them all is buying a pre-owned vehicle that is around 4-6 years old, is a great value with reasonable mileage, and you pay cash. This option completely eliminates the car payment, gives you dependability, and affords you another 5-6 years to save up for the next one! It will still look nice, get you to and from places safely, and not cause you a big headache or leave your wallet with a massive dent in it!

The Big Four: Tackling those necessary expenses including housing, food, clothing & utilities.

Clothing & Utilities

Now it is time to examine the big four essential expenses, especially focusing on housing and food. Clothing and utilities are certainly important and necessary items. Most of us do not need new clothes at this point. I challenge you to walk into your closet right now and I bet there are nearly ten things that you haven't worn in over a year. Even when we update styles we can do so at a fairly low cost. If you are a frequent flyer to the mall or that one button express shopping on Amazon, this might be an area that you focus on with more intentionality. Yes, most guys don't buy as many clothes as women do, however I have a wife who is a fashionista so I know what that is all about! Not buying in excess is key and sticking to your clothing budget whatever you set that at is important. Heat and electricity, that good old National Grid utility bill is something you cannot escape. No need to live in the forest and break out the logs and matches. However, there are options out there depending upon the state that you live in, where you can utilize clean and renewable energy from solar and wind power suppliers. These companies work directly with National Grid and offer cheaper, yet still fully reliable supplies of energy. I made the switch a while ago and it has saved me over 20% per month over the past few years. My utility bill has never been lower and I even have a furnace that is not energy efficient from my home built in the 1960s! Don't worry, old faithful is still blowing out the hot air, but the savings in making the switch to clean energy has been huge. Not to mention it is helping the environment. The best part is that they don't have to install anything new. You won't even know you made the switch, except for that bill bottom line will be drastically lower! My last suggestion on the heating and electricity front is to get a Nest thermostat or some other tech savvy system that will cost a couple hundred dollars up front, but will save you thousands over the long haul. That way you can adjust your thermostat from anywhere in the world. Why pay to crank the heat when nobody is home for hours each day.

Food

What's for dinner? The typical question of the day. For many of us it will be a quick stop to grab some take out, or to pick up a pizza on the way home from work. Maybe you are meeting up with your friends at that nice new restaurant that just opened up downtown. And for those of you, like me, you are taking the quintessential deep dive into the refrigerator to explore the options to cook up a meal. Why is nothing jumping out at you out of that fridge? Regardless of your choice, we all need to eat. Food is a necessity. When I was a kid growing up I cannot tell you how many times I heard my dad harp on the cost of food. He was constantly verbalizing how much he spent at the grocery store. He was part of the savings fan club so he religiously clipped coupons back in those days. My household growing up was always looking for ways to save, especially on meals. At the time, I didn't think about it too much because we always ate well and what was on the table tasted pretty good! After college, once I got my own apartment, I soon realized that food was a big time budget line item. It finally made sense to me why one of my dad's famous sayings was, "You will spend more money on food than anything else in your lifetime." He was right. Over the course of one's life it is estimated that the average American will spend nearly $300,000 on food for a single person. That's a lot of dough and no I am not speaking of the kind that comes in the square box with cheese and sauce on it! According to reports from *Business Insider*, the range for monthly grocery bill expenses of the average American household (of 2.5 people) is between $314-$516 monthly. That is not too bad! My household monthly grocery bill comes in at around $450 and we are strictly plant based (vegan). So, things tend to be a little more expensive the healthier one eats. The big kicker when it comes to food is usually not the grocery bill, it is money spent on eating out! Don't worry, I am not saying you will never eat out again, it is just a huge factor to consider because it adds up really quickly. Reports revealed that the average person in the U.S. spends over $250 per month on food outside of their household. This includes take out, ordering meals, and restaurant visits. Not to mention, nearly $100 spent on coffee per month is often added to the cost. I'm glad I am not a huge coffee guy! I say hold the latte, well at least make it at home. The extra few minutes is not going to kill you, but what it will do is make a killing for your bank account. Did you know that if you were to simply eat in or even cut your monthly restaurant visits in half you would have another $100-$150 per month to spend. For some of you out there it would be way more! Oh yeah and that $25 per week Starbucks habit you have established, that can go bye bye too! That's another $1,200 per year you drink in coffee that can be made at home for a fraction of the cost. Combine the two and pay attention to your grocery expenses by utilizing coupons and shopping smart, now you changed your situation in a drastic manner! Look out, here comes a walking Mr. or Mrs. Money Bags! We are talking about upwards of $300-$500 more per month or possibly $6,000 a year! How would you feel about getting a $6,000 raise? I know that would make me happy. What about you? The craziest part is that this need, namely food, being met in a different manner by cutting down expenses, has just freed up thousands upon thousands of dollars. What is even better is when you learn how to maximize earning potential and turn your excessive, undisciplined, and nonchalant spending on food into investments that over a 25-30 year period can net over $1,000,000! Yeah that is right. The math doesn't lie! If I take $500 a month X 12 months that gives me $6,000 for the year. $6,000 X 30 years will bring me in at $180,000 spent during that time period. That number alone is staggering! But when you put it in an investment account for those thirty years at about 9% interest, it can balloon in your favor to equate to a cool million! No wonder why Albert Einstein said, "Compound interest is the eighth wonder of the world!" To learn more about this and investments, we will turn to that chapter in the text. But before we move on there is one more big essential expense necessary to discuss.

Housing

It's time to put your hands up and raise the roof! Finally, we are going to talk about housing. This is by far and wide the largest expense you will have in your budget each month, if it is not, you have some real adjusting to do. For you who are still living home with your parents, you are the sole exception. Or are you? As for the rare few who might claim their car is their home, you better be driving a Mobile Home. All jokes aside, according to rentcafe.com the average rent in the U.S. as of January 2020 was $1,463, while the typical mortgage payment came in at a median rate of $1,500. Interestingly enough, these are around the same number. You might be a homeowner or if you are not, chances are you are renting. I have a great deal of experience with both realms. Either way, this is a big ticket item. Once you become debt free, I suggest saving enough for a decent down payment and getting into a home. Many financial experts would suggest the same. Rent for many people is like piling up your money in the center of the room and lighting it on fire. There is nothing to show for it, keep this in the back of your mind. As for now we will tackle some housing costs before we get into utilizing our home as an investment.   So how can we lower the cost of living each month? We all need four walls around us and a roof over our heads. Well, for starters, if you are single and don't have a family, you can always share rent costs with roommates. That is a term in the financial world called house hacking. By splitting up the rental cost amongst two or three others, this will lower your monthly payment exceptionally. Maybe you have children and that is not an option, you can shop around to find a lower cost property to move into where the rent is cheaper. For those home owners out there, I know what you are thinking, I signed a thirty year loan with the mortgage company at a fixed rate. There is always the option to refinance at a lower interest rate or sell your home when the time is right and move into something that is more affordable in a different area that has a lower cost of living. For those who work in the city and live there, try to get into a section that is still safe, yet less expensive or commute in. Paying top dollar to live right in the middle of everything might not be worth it after all. No, this decision with housing unlike cable, cell phones, and even food is far from easy. Yet, it is worth considering and exploring the options. Saving a few hundred dollars or more each month could be life changing for you and your financial future.

Little changes like making your lunch and bringing it to work each day, eating leftovers, taking your money from that food envelope to the grocery store, and not having to have the new iPhone every time it comes out will provide you with some serious cash! Implement a couple of these strategies this month and then one or two more in the next few months to come. Little changes make a difference and big changes a monumental one.   Slowly, but surely, your disposable income and cash flow will radically change. It is the day to day expenses that often add up the most. How we live our lives on the regular and what we spend our money on each month will either add fuel to the fire and burn up our accounts, or ignite a new outlook that includes a choice filled future. It is totally up to you, but you can no longer claim that you didn't know. So what will you choose and what are you waiting for? It is time to make some adjustments.

CHALLENGE #3: **Pick at least two of the categories discussed in this chapter and implement them to lower your expenses!**

I understand that this may not be a fun challenge for most of you, however it is the one that will put the green in your pocket and place you on a rocket toward your goals. Nothing in life is permanent so this doesn't have to be a forever change. However, remember that sacrifice is necessary to win with money. Along with your budgeting, you are continuing to rebuild and reshape what is normal in your life. The benefits of doing so can be exponential based on what you do with that extra money that you will have.

"Baby steps count as long as you are going forward. You add them all up and one day you look back and you will be surprised at where you might get to."

-Chris Gardner

CHAPTER 5:
More Baby Steps into the Future

Baby Step 3: Save 3-6 months expenses for an emergency fund

Time for another step. At this point in our journey together, we have made it to baby step number three. Coming off of the most recent and tragic Coronavirus pandemic which took the world by storm and attacked out of nowhere, this next topic has extreme value and weight for every person. Whether you are new to taking finances seriously or are the most experienced of them all, being prepared for "rainy days" is vital. The tragedy that our country and world has undergone which caused everything to come to an abrupt halt, stopped the economy, and left millions of people unemployed during months of quarantine, has been significant. During the mass shutdown that took place during the COVID-19 era so many people struggled immensely and this new age great depression became much too familiar for us all. Something that "never happened before," indeed did take place. As a result, a multitude of people in our country could not make ends meet, businesses had to close some permanently, people lost their homes, and bank accounts were drained to the last penny. This is all the more reason why a fully fledged emergency fund is no longer a good idea, but a necessity. When I teach my financial class on Tuesday nights, I have a great time with the students in the room. Age ranges run the gamut from 18 being my youngest student to my oldest being in his upper 80s! When we get to baby step three in the program, I tend to look around the room at the faces of those gathered to estimate how many actually have this fully loaded emergency fund. In most cases less than 20% of them did prior to the Coronavirus pandemic. However, that number has increased significantly as tragedy has woken many people up. It is okay if you do not have that full emergency fund at this very moment to tap into, however we want to get you there as quickly as possible. We all saw and experienced to varying degrees, the heartache that ensued as a result of such an unpredictable disaster during the Coronavirus saga. Let's be prepared for all emergencies no matter what form they might come our way in.

Saving three to six months worth of expenses might not seem that crazy, but for most of us it will take a while. We are talking about covering the absolute necessities of those big four (housing, food, clothing, utilities) and probably the minimal cell phone plan, as well as health insurance. Outside of that, everything else would be a want. In other words, if you were to lose your job today, would you be okay living on what you have in the bank for the next half of a year? Being furloughed, fired or laid off is scary. Chances are, you are not and could not survive this well if you don't have an emergency fund. In addition, unemployment benefits will only provide a certain amount per week for half a year based on the state you live in. Take New York for example, a maximum of $504 is paid out for unemployment, many people getting far less. To calculate the rate of pay, the Department of Labor (NYSDOL) determines one's benefit amount by dividing a person's earnings for the highest paid quarter over the base period by 26. So for you who are doing really well or have a middle of the road job, $504 doesn't go too far, trust me. Skeptics out there might be thinking, it is a very slim chance for *me* to lose *my* job. I like your confidence, but it can happen to all of us. COVID-19 left me unemployed, but because of my emergency fund and not having any debt I was beyond okay. Nothing really changed for my household during those horrible times. I am grateful to be able to say so, however it wasn't luck. It was all about being prepared and making the chances run in my favor by putting in the hard and unglamorous work of saving the money. Rainy days come, let me tell you, and when they do they tend to blast through in dramatic fashion. You heard the saying, "When it rains, it pours." Well, the emergency fund is to safeguard you against being flooded out and knocked backward into more debt. If you are prepared, that cannot and will not happen, but failing to prepare is indeed a recipe for disaster.

So how should one start out saving for their rainy day fund? Well, you can begin by taking any extra money that you have after all the bills and budget is paid out and put that into a savings account that you do not touch. Again we will discuss the savings options in detail in the future, but the main thing is to put some money away. Growing up in the 1990s I remember the multitude of infomercials including the one that kept coming up around the holiday season regarding the crock pot. The woman or man would be on there in the kitchen and put some kind of roast in, close the top, and say emphatically, "Set it and forget it." There are numerous money tactics and techniques that apply to this, one of which is the emergency fund. Similar to your $1,000 baby step one, small emergency fund, this fully fledged fund is for just that, emergencies. You can use the $1,000 to provide a jump start for your large emergency fund. I totally endorse that choice. This is what my wife and I did once we became debt free. Month after month we added to the pot, until we accumulated the six months worth of expenses based on our budget. That is now set aside and hopefully never has to be used again. In our case we had to dip in there a little during the Coronavirus quarantine when I lost my job, but we quickly replenished it and now it's there for when it might decide to rain again.

Lea was a single mother of three. She was a hard working hair-dresser and a successful one at that. She was always able to provide for her family and ensured that her kids ate well, dressed nice, and did not have any needs. Unfortunately, her salon was shut down during the COVID-19 pandemic. Lea was laid off and unemployment benefits were significantly delayed due to the increase of people applying at the time. She greatly struggled to put food on her table and keep the lights on. As she cried herself to sleep each night, I bet she wished she would have taken the time to save and fund an emergency account. She was mortified that she had to ask her parents for help. Lea had no other choice or her kids would be living in darkness inside their two bedroom apartment. After she returned to work, when the dust settled and the salon reopened, Lea made some changes. The first for her was saving any and all tips she earned toward an emergency fund. Before you knew it, Lea had a full emergency fund ready to be utilized. She now sleeps better at night knowing that a tidal wave of disaster cannot and will not throw her family into a tailspin in the future. My hope is that you can learn from Lea's story and others that you have heard of. Conviction on this one is key. Having an emergency fund is a critical decision that will pad your financial walls and give extra support during times of need.

The furnace goes, my washer and dryer stopped working, or the transmission blows on the car. All of these are examples of when the emergency fund will come in handy. The emergency won't feel like an emergency at all because you will be prepared and not scared of the bill that comes your way. There will no longer be the feeling or thought of how will I ever afford this? No, instead, you will remember, oh yeah, I have that $10,000 saved. This will lighten the load and burden, making it much easier to draw on that account than try to figure out what you will do. After you take the money out and pay for the unforeseen expense, I suggest doing what my wife and I did, replenish it. Take the next few paychecks or months to systematically reload that emergency fund so you are ready for whatever life throws at you.

CHALLENGE #4: Load up your emergency fund.

The thing that I hate the most is seeing people I advise kicking themselves for not heeding sound advice. I am then left with the thought running through my mind, "I told you so." I cannot stand that. Take the emergency fund challenge seriously. Do yourself and your household a favor and start building it up brick by brick and dollar by dollar. Fully fund this account to complete baby step three so when the curve balls at life are thrown at you, you can take the approach of a cool customer and fend them off. No problem baby! If you need to dangle a little incentive carrot on the end of the stick to help you stay motivated to get to the full six months to solidify this fund, I am cool with that. Treat yourself to a nice dinner out or that new pair of shoes when you close out that emergency fund account and deposit the last dollar. After all, you are now debt free and have an ample size amount of cash in the bank. You can afford to pat yourself on the back. Small rewards for reaching goals is a good thing. Now it is time to get ready for the fun stuff and make some real money!

"Investing is not nearly as difficult as it looks. Successful investing involves doing a few things right and avoiding serious mistakes."

– John Bogle

CHAPTER 6: Investments 101

Tackling Taxation, Utilizing one's Paycheck, & Investing Money for the Future.

There are many things that excite people and give them a rush of energy. For me, investments jack me up and tend to be something that creates such a big time high just talking about them. Seeing my investments or those of my students and advisees pan out is amazing. Interestingly enough, when I was a whole lot younger I was super conservative with money. When I finally realized the value of a dollar and got my spending under control, I simply wanted to save it by putting cash in the bank. Saving is really good, don't get me wrong, but there is a far better way. I had this notion that I worked too hard to "gamble" my money away in the stock market or take a risk that I wasn't sure I would see come to full fruition. Stowing money away in a savings account was a safe bet and I was guaranteed I would not lose any. Or so I thought. What do you mean you say? Well, at the moment that this book was written, average inflation was 2-3% per year, as a result, when your money sits in a savings account it grows only if you put more money in. That is normal you are thinking. Actually, I am sorry to say that you are wrong if that thought came to mind. Don't worry, I was wrong back in the day as well. I didn't realize that the 0.05% interest that my bank was paying on my money sitting in my savings account was costing me 2-3% every year due to inflation. Let alone, I had no clue of the investment vehicles that were out there for every customer of all ages, incomes, and sizes that could be driven. From the most risky of them all, to the safest nest egg bet, you can pick what you feel comfortable with. The thing about it is, if you remain sitting on the sideline, you will never excel. You cannot win the game unless you play. So the first step is getting in the game and that is where baby step number four comes in. Believe me, far too many people are kicking themselves down the line wishing they got started sooner.

Baby Step 4: Invest 15% of your income each month

Most economic experts, including the likes of Warren Buffet, Dave Ramsey, and others suggest investing at least 15% of your take home pay each month. Now that you are debt free, have a fully loaded emergency fund, and are crushing life on a budget, it is time to empower your money to maximize its potential. Like I said and cannot say enough, there is nothing that gets me more excited than sharing with people the multitude of options accessible when it comes to investing. This is definitely the fun side of finances, especially when we see our accounts grow at an exponential rate. The first area of investing we will cover is planning for your future and retirement. There are a number of avenues and ways to do so. After discussing these, it will be critical to discuss other investment vehicles that are out there to access and use in order to get the biggest bang for your buck.

Saving & Investing for Retirement

Retirement. She was sitting on the beach with her feet in the sand as the warm sun shone down on her. She read her book and felt the cool ocean breeze coming off of those aqua blue Caribbean waters. He was off on another adventure. Seated in the plane next to his wife and a number of friends, soon they would be in Europe. He imagined lunch near the Spanish Steps or Trevi Fountain, tours of the Colosseum, and taking in the sites of the French Riviera. She was excited to be able to hop on a plane and visit her grandchildren up north for Christmas and then head back down to the Sunshine State to escape time away from the snowy cold weather. The point that all hard working people long to get to is retirement. At 31 years old it is about three decades away for me. Or is it? The average age of a person who reaches retirement in the U.S. is 62 years old. That is the norm, it is what is expected, and it is what we have to do. So deal with it! Get up, go to work, come home, eat dinner, go to sleep. Repeat this process and run on this hamster wheel for 40 some odd years and you will reach retirement. To me this is ludicrous. Why do what everyone else does and is unhappy doing? Don't get me wrong, if you love your job and want to work doing what you enjoy until you are 70 or even older, be my guest. I am willing to bet that the majority of people out there, if they didn't have to work, today would be their very last day! So you're telling me there is another option? Yes, I am. There is more than one other option. For those of you who are very ambitious and desire to really take this to the next level, I suggest you acquire a copy of the book *Playing with FIRE* by Scott Reickens, as well as the text *Choose FI: Your Blueprint to Financial Independence*. These books will lay out how to achieve what is called FIRE (Financial Independence Retire Early) and outline the ways that you can reach this in order to not have to work through sacrifice, saving and investing upwards of 50-70% or more of your income to get to a place where working is optional. More on this a bit later. For the mainstream reader out there, let's walk through saving for retirement so that you have a great nest egg built up to draw upon by the time you reach 59.5 years of age. At the moment that is the legal age you can withdraw money from retirement funds in the U.S. without penalty.

To begin, there are a number of investment vehicles one can choose when planning for and saving for their retirement. When I use the word save in this section, it is more closely aligned to investing. We are by no means putting our money underneath a mattress or sticking it in a bank account for the next decades to come. That is a horrible idea. Don't do that! The vehicles that are out there for you and I to utilize include and are not limited to IRAs, Roth IRAs, 403Bs, 401Ks, 457s, Life Cycle Funds, Stocks, Bonds, ETFS, index Funds, Mutual Funds, and Real Estate. Okay, Dan, you lost me. What do all of these mean? I had no clue what all of this financial jargon meant until I began reading great books such as Chris Hogan's *Retire Inspired*, *Everyday Millionaires,* and Benjamin Graham's *Intelligent Investor*. Don't worry, we will unpack it all and make it as simple as possible to understand. The main thing is that you begin to stow away 15% of your income each month and allow compound interest to work it's magic by saving/investing.

One of my desires is to travel to Asia in the near future and explore the beauty that exists in the jungles of Taiwan. I can imagine myself riding on an elephant or taking a jeep safari where we get to see all that mother nature has to offer. There is a guarantee that when I am there amongst many beautiful and amazing creatures, I will see lots and lots of bamboo. Bamboo is a plant that is essential for the vitality and growth of the rainforest, as well as the survival of the animals that live there. The thing that most people do not know about bamboo is that it takes upward of a couple of years before the stem and shoot breaks through the soil. I am no botanist by any means, but I did my research! The roots of the bamboo plant run so deep into the ground and it is extremely slow developing at first. However, once the bamboo plant busts through the initial layer of dirt, the growth is wild and excels at an incredibly high rate! Compound interest is very similar to this. It takes a while to get started, but then the growth begins to happen on top of more growth. Before you know it, look out! You will have a whole damn forest that is wild and out of control. That is what I am talking about!

When it comes to our money and investments, nobody will ever be upset with that kind of exponential increase. More is better, I can promise you that.

Perceiving the Basics: Gross Income vs. Net Income and how AGI is calculated

Before we dive deeper into the retirement game plan and dissect each of the most popular and available vehicles out there for the average investor at least on a macro level, it is crucial that we explain some basics. There are a variety of terms you have most likely heard, but might have been like me, and were wondering what they actually meant. Every time you get paid, cha-ching, money ends up going into your account. This is good. However, as you know, if you pay attention to the actual paycheck, there are numerous things that are deducted and the salary or hourly wage that you make at your workplace ends up being a lot lower than the initial amount. This is due to a number of factors including taxation, health insurance, workers compensation, unemployment, and others. Gross income refers to what your employer says he or she will pay you for the work you do at that particular job place. I like to think of gross, literally nasty, because none of us actually takes home that larger dollar amount, although it would be nice! What we are left with is nasty in comparison, well hopefully it's not that bad.

Let's look at an example so it is easier to understand and break down what I mean. We will take a worker and call her Chloe. Chloe works for XCompany and at the end of her two week pay period she makes $2,100 gross pay. This is based on her overall salary for the year of $54,600. Since there are 12 months in the year, which equates to 52 weeks and she gets paid every two weeks, that breaks down to 26 times Chloe is paid. So that is why each time her gross pay is $2,100. The thing is, that as you know, this is not what she will bring home. What Chloe will bring home is called net pay or adjusted gross income (AGI). Your net income or take home pay, which actually goes into your bank account if you have direct deposit, is your gross pay minus all of the deductions we discussed above and any withholdings from your paycheck due to tax purposes. In addition, net pay also must factor in any retirement contributions you are making. The latter is a good type of deduction we will discuss at length momentarily. Your net income, which is often called take-home pay, is the bottom line, total amount that your paycheck or Chloe's paycheck in this case is written for. So if Chloe cashes the check, or if she uses direct deposit, $2,100 will not be going into her account. A general broad rule of thumb I like to use when configuring gross income to net (take home pay) calculation is to subtract 22% to account for taxes and another few percentage points for the other deductions. In some cases your tax rate will be less than that 22% (see below) and for others a bit more depending on your income level. So I figure for the average middle class worker making between $40K-$85K per year (gross) based on IRS guidelines and other factors, to configure about a 30% reduction in your paycheck from gross pay to take home (net pay). That gives you a roundabout idea of what you will most likely be bringing home. So for Chloe, XCompany paid her $2,100, we subtract roughly 30% to account for taxes, deductions and all other adjustments and her net pay that she takes home is looking more like an approximate amount of $1,470 every two weeks. Again, this is before she contributed anything to her retirement account. So what I like to do before I am going into a new job, negotiating my salary or hourly wage, discussing raises with the boss, and/or talking about income with my employer, is to think about how much I am actually going to be taking home every pay period. That is the amount that matters most. A $50,000 salary might seem great, but in actuality it is going to end up being more like $35,000 or so annual rate after everything is taken out of it. Just some food for thought.

Factoring in Taxation & Adjustments Continued

When it comes time to file your taxes, I suggest that you refer to the latest government guidelines for your specific state and that you speak to your tax representative who helps you with this endeavor. Ask them the specific questions that you might have about withholdings and dependents that you are claiming on your tax return, as each person's is different depending on their situation and the state they live in. There are a thousand different scenarios and I am certainly not going to try to outline them all, nor is that relevant for your situation. However it is important for every person to understand the taxation and adjustments that take place on each paycheck. It will factor into your adjusted gross income (AGI), which we referenced above, which ultimately impacts how much money you actually see in your wallet. In addition, it is significant to know that as of 2020 for an individual tax filing, there was a $12,400 standard deduction, for a married couple filing jointly, they were allowed a deduction of $24,800, while a head of the household was allowed to deduct $18,650 off the top when filing taxes based on yearly income. Basically, what that means is that when Chloe files she has to say I made X amount this year, subtract the $12,400 from it and she will be taxed then at the appropriate adjusted income amount. The more you make, unfortunately the more you are taxed. However, there are ways to shield or shelter your money from getting taken by greedy Uncle Sam. This is one of the benefits of various retirement accounts and real estate investing. For more in depth and the latest up to date tax amounts regulations please visit **https://taxfoundation.org/2020-tax-brackets/** as it will include everything and all the numbers that you are looking for. As for Chloe, who is single, she would be taxed at the 22% rate since her salary is between $40,125 and $85,525. However, we had to account for her other deductions from her paycheck as well. In other words the estimated 30% I suggested previously could be a tad higher when calculating her net pay, but it gives us a ballpark number. Not everyone out there is like me and enjoys crunching numbers, let alone calculations to the last penny. The bottom line is, if you make above $40,000 in gross pay you will be tagged at the 22% rate or higher, meanwhile if your income is lower than that you will be hit with a 12% rate. This will only be lower if you make less than $10,000. So figure on 25-30% coming out of your bi-weekly paycheck for starters. Some detailed and specific tax tables and rates have been provided for you below so that you can configure where you are at in terms of AGI and what you will be required to hand over to Uncle Sam throughout the year and on doom's day each April. As long as you have enough coming out of your paycheck each month, you won't have to write a fat check to the government. The goal is to get as close to $0. I realize many of you might enjoy receiving a nice tax check in the mail, however this is essentially loaning your money at 0% to the Feds and State. If we can avoid this, let's do it. The moral of the story is to become more knowledgeable about your paycheck, taxation, and withholdings. This will only come in handy as you grow your finances and do everything possible to get to the highest point or maximum level that is allowed at your tax bracket.

Tax Tables as of 2020:

Table 1. 2020 Tax Brackets and Rates

Rate	For Single Individuals, Taxable Income Over	For Married Individuals Filing Joint Returns, Taxable Income Over	For Heads of Households, Taxable Income Over
10%	$0	$0	$0
12%	$9,875	$19,750	$14,100
22%	$40,125	$80,250	$53,700
24%	$85,525	$171,050	$85,500
32%	$163,300	$326,600	$163,300
35%	$207,350	$414,700	$207,350
37%	$518,400	$622,050	$518,400

Source: Internal Revenue Service

Table 2. 2020 Standard Deduction

Filing Status	Deduction Amount
Single	$12,400
Married Filing Jointly	$24,800
Head of Household	$18,650

Source: Internal Revenue Service

AMT exemptions phase out at 25 cents per dollar earned once taxpayer AMTI hits a certain threshold. In 2020, the exemption will start phasing out at $518,400 in AMTI for single filers and $1,036,800 for married taxpayers filing jointly (Table 4).

Table 4. 2020 Alternative Minimum Tax Exemption Phaseout Thresholds

Filing Status	Threshold
Single Individuals	$518,400
Married Filing Jointly	$1,036,800

Source: Internal Revenue Service

Table 5. 2020 Earned Income Tax Credit Parameters

Filing Status		No Children	One Child	Two Children	Three or More Children
Single or Head of Household	Income at Max Credit	$7,030	$10,540	$14,800	$14,800
	Maximum Credit	$538	$3,584	$5,920	$6,660
	Phaseout Begins	$8,790	$19,330	$19,330	$19,330
	Phaseout Ends (Credit Equals Zero)	$15,820	$41,756	$47,440	$50,954
Married Filing Jointly	Income at Max Credit	$7,030	$10,540	$14,800	$14,800
	Maximum Credit	$538	$3,584	$5,920	$6,660
	Phaseout Begins	$14,680	$25,220	$25,220	$25,220
	Phaseout Ends (Credit Equals Zero)	$21,710	$47,646	$53,330	$56,844

Source: Internal Revenue Service

The Difference Between an IRA and a Roth IRA

In the world of finance there is a lot of jargon, technical terminology thrown around, and code language. Do not be alarmed or worried if you do not know what all of these mean. My hope is to break it down to you so that it is more understandable and easier to digest. The most important thing is knowing what each investment vehicle offers and how it can benefit you in the long run, mid game, or short term. For now, in this section, we are focusing on the marathon race, the long haul. It is back to that analogy of the crock pot. A slow and steady meal simmers for hours. At the conclusion of a long time period, this meal often tends to be the most tasty of them all and doesn't require a ton of work. The key here is that it does take time. The likelihood of burning food in a crockpot is very slim, while flash frying in the pan has great risk if we do not pay extra close attention minute by minute. Some investors would compare day trading stocks to this flash fry method, meanwhile the crockpot is the IRA or Roth IRA route. So what is an IRA anyway? Well, the three letters stand for an Individual Retirement Account. Each person can choose to begin one pretty much at any time once they turn 18 years of age and it can be drawn upon starting at age 59.5. These are simply regulations that the government has put on such accounts. For many of you out there whose employer does not offer any retirement account plan, this is one of the best options for you to put money away for years down the road. It is very simple to open up such an account. By contacting any investment firm or going online, you can begin one with as little as $100 in many cases. The most important thing to know about traditional IRAs is that they utilize money that is under the category of pre-tax dollars. What this boils down to is that you make contributions before you pay taxes on the money that is being invested. This can come in the form of going into your IRA directly as a deduction from your paycheck (AGI) in a direct deposit fashion if you wish. You are not taxed on the money now, but later on. Down the road when you withdraw the funds during retirement, then at that point you will pay Uncle Sam based on your income tax level and rate. Another important thing to know about traditional IRAs is that the most you can legally contribute as of 2020 per year was $6,000. A big benefit of the traditional IRA is that there is no income limit. So you can make as much money as possible and still contribute up to that $6,000 amount and can keep contributing until you are 70 ½ years old. If you desire to withdraw money before reaching 59.5 years of age, you will be penalized for doing so. You will be dinged with a 10% penalty, on top of your current income rate for taxation at the time of an early withdrawal from an IRA account.

ROTH IRA

A Roth IRA, my personal favorite investment vehicle for retirement, outside of the employer matching program, which we will discuss in the next section, allows you to contribute upwards of $6,000 per year, post-tax. This means that your entire nest egg will grow tax free as you already paid taxes on the money before the contribution amount went into the account. What this means is that when you withdraw the funds during retirement, you will be free and in the clear. If you are 50 years of age or over, you are allowed to contribute $7,000 per year, as the government allows for an extra $1,000 to help people catch up accumulating their retirement growth. The downside to the Roth IRA is that there are income level restrictions for contribution eligibility. Based on federal regulations with the IRS (as of 2020), an individual tax filer can make a full contribution if their modified adjusted gross income is less than $124,000. If their modified adjusted gross income is more than $124,000 but less than $139,000, a partial contribution is allowed. For the sake of brevity and to make this as simple to comprehend as possible, I am not going to get into how to calculate partial contributions at the moment. However, if you wish to learn more about those specific numbers the most up to date information can be found on ***irs.gov/retirement***. Another thing to keep in mind is there is something called a back door Roth, which allows a person to contribute money as an IRA (pre-tax), roll it directly over into a Roth IRA account by paying the tax on it and still be able to contribute the maximum amount even if they are above the income level cap. Again, for the sake of the majority of the audience, this is probably not applicable. However, if it is and you are making over $124,000 as an individual, good for you! That is awesome. Hopefully we will all get there or exceed that amount as we continue to learn and grow with our finances. For married couples, the limits are a bit higher if you are filing jointly. You can each have your own IRA and/or Roth IRA as well. Couples can make a full contribution as long as their modified adjusted gross income is less than $196,000. If you are over that amount, but less than $206,000 as a married couple, a partial contribution is allowed. For those working out there who do not have a work retirement plan, I suggest along with the other experts out there that you set up both types of accounts.

Beginning at age 72, the government is going to require you to start withdrawing money from these accounts and you are not allowed to keep funding them. But my hope is that you will be long since retired and have a great net worth by then, so that piece of information will be irrelevant anyway. Similar to a traditional IRA, if you choose to withdraw funds early, there is usually a penalty of 10% or higher on the interest you made on your investment. However, the initial principal amount that was contributed can be withdrawn without penalty or taxation from the Roth account at any time even before you are 59.5 years of age. I do not recommend this, as it will negate maximum growth potential by utilizing compound interest. However, if it was a major emergency and that emergency fund you saved doesn't cover all the damages, this is a last resort option. As you can see, contributing 15% of your take home pay is a great place to start during baby step four. Working on investing toward retirement is important. We will run through some numbers that will indeed excited you, but first we need to examine some other options in the world of investments.

"The philosophy of the rich and the poor is this: the rich invest their money and spend what is left. The poor spend their money and invest what is left."

– Robert Kiyosaki

CHAPTER 7:
Unpacking Investments Over the Long Haul

401Ks, 403(b)s, 457s, Deferred Compensation, & More

Another beneficial vehicle that many job places offer is a retirement plan or program for their employees. This is different from a full pension, as these types of retirement options are unfortunately almost non-existent. For state or federal employees, depending on what state you live in, the pension program may still exist. Many times an employer that pays out a pension also offers deferred compensation, which is very similar to the retirement plans we will be discussing in this section. When I began my investing in retirement nearly a decade ago, I had no clue what the difference was between a 401K and a Roth IRA or what these names and numbers meant. Essentially, the number associated with the investment retirement account is simply the tax code to help the IRS determine what deductions are acceptable for the one filing and to configure how much we owe Uncle Sam. Employer plans most often fall into the category of a 401K, 403(b) or 457, the latter many times referred to as a deferred compensation plan. The major difference between the three plans is the type of employer sponsoring the plan. 401K plans are offered by private companies that are for-profit, while the 403(b) plan is only available to nonprofit organizations and government employers. The 457 (deferred comp) is for state and local government workers and some nonprofits. So if you are an educator or work a job for a nonprofit or the Feds you most likely are going to have a 403(b), more localized government workers will have a 457, and typically everyone else whose employer offers a retirement program falls under the 401K umbrella. The amount that one can contribute to these plans is significantly greater than the IRA plans we discussed in the previous section. As of 2020, the limit for the 401K, 403(b), and 457 plans was $19,500 per year, until you reach age 50 where the contribution max increases to $26,000. All of these plans are pre-tax retirement investments, meaning when the money goes in it is not taxed at the moment of entry, but taxation happens later on when funds are withdrawn. The same age stipulation is applicable for the majority of these plans, being set at 59.5 to withdraw funds without penalty. There are a few stipulations depending on the government's regulations for retirees who are police, fire, emergency responders, or military personnel. The best and most significant part of many employer retirement plans is when they have a matching program. A retirement employer match means that the company you work for will match, dollar for dollar, what you contribute to the plan up to a certain amount. This is FREE MONEY!!! Let me say that again, free money! You must take advantage of this if your workplace offers such compensation. It is part of the benefits package your job comes with and if you are unsure if your employer offers this, take time to speak to your HR representative to find out about this right away. Who doesn't like free money? Now, you may be thinking, there must be a catch. Like all things in life, nothing is totally free. Well, in this case, the employer retirement match is totally free. However, the one caveat is something called becoming vested. What this means is that each company has the ability to require you to work at their firm for a designated length of time that they set, before you have complete and total access to the matched funds in your retirement account. Learn what this vesting period requires so you know exactly when the matching funds will be totally yours to keep.

Breaking Down an Example of Matching Retirement Plans

Let's take a moment and use Chloe working for XCompany to explain things and break them down a bit further. Chloe's XCompany is a for-profit private company, so she has access to a 401K plan. She is excited because she is now debt free and is in baby step four ready to invest in her future. Chloe has learned that her company offers an employer match on her 401K plan. This is great! Chloe discusses her options with her HR representative and finds out that her employer match is 6%! Wow! She then finds out that in order for her to be fully vested with XCompany, she needs to have worked for her employer for at least three years. The good news is that Chloe has been working there for the past four years, so she is already fully vested since she met the requirement for that amount of time with her workplace. Even though she hadn't begun contributing yet, she can start today. As long as Chloe puts in 6% of her annual salary into the 401K, the XCompany will match that amount. So on her $54,600 annual salary amount, she would have to contribute 6% which equates to $3,276 per year or $126 per paycheck. XCompany will then put in the matching 6%, another $3,276 free dollars annually, bringing Chloe in at a total contribution of $6,522 for the year. She would then have another 3% to contribute if she wants to hit that magic 15% threshold that is suggested. She can do so in this same 401K plan by bumping her contribution from 6% to 9% or she could open a Roth IRA or regular IRA if she prefers. Even if Chloe decided to max out her 401K and invest the limit of $19,500 in 2020, her employer is only going to match the first 6% of her contribution. But that is okay, again it is free money. The good news is that every year that Chloe gets a raise or each time her salary increases, the total amount her employer contributes will also increase. This is the power of the growing income. Although the percentage (6% set rate) stays the same, with increased income comes increased free money. If Chloe were to merely invest her 6% and the employer matching 6% alone, for the next 30 years, and her salary never increased at all, she would have contributed a total of $111,780 of her own money. At this point, XCompany would have provided her an additional $111,780. When combined, that is a grand total of $223,560 in total retirement investments. You are probably thinking, not too bad for investing $126 per paycheck, right? On the other hand, a quarter of a million dollars is definitely not going to be enough to be able to retire fully by the year 2050!! So what now Dan, all of this investment is for nothing and I have to work even longer anyway? I'm out! Wait a moment, we still haven't factored in the most important part of all, compound interest. Remember that bamboo I was referring to at the beginning of the previous chapter? Recall how it took a number of years to even start breaking the soil's surface. Then it was growing wildly and out of control. After we factor in compound interest and use a moderate rate of return of 8.75% (the S&P500 has gotten 9.8% since 1928), Chloe's nest egg of $111,780 of her own contributions combined with what her employer matched will have grown to a whopping $1,008,204.57. Now that is more of what I am talking about! If she bumps her own contribution up from the 6% amount to the 9% amount, that is just a 3% increase, or $63 per paycheck, that final nest egg will be even higher, growing to over $1,260,000. So adding another $63 per paycheck because of compound interest will mean an additional quarter of a million to your retirement account. The name of the game is getting in early so that time can continue to compound and your money grows on top of your money. We will dissect this factor and wonder of compound interest even more later on.

457 Plans aka Deferred Comp

Lastly, deferred compensation (457) plans work very similar to the above 401K or 403(b) plans. In addition to your pension that is set up with your government employer, you can contribute additional funds to be utilized just like Chloe did with her 401K. This is great because the more money you have saved for retirement the better. The other great benefit is that since all of this money is contributed pre-tax, you can write this off on your taxes every year. For Chloe and others out there, this means that your AGI will be a lot lower and when the standard deduction is plugged in your income you show that it is taxable will be less, meaning there is a good likelihood that you will be getting money back from Uncle Sam. And we all like receiving that check in the mail during the springtime. For those who have pension programs and deferred compensation options, say police officers for instance, there is one more great benefit. Since you are required to work for 20 years and then can draw on your pension, you can also begin collecting money from your deferred comp plan well before 59.5 years of age. In many cases, depending upon the state and regulations, you can have full access to the 457/deferred comp money at this point of retirement also. Why is this important to know. Well, if you begin working at 25 and two decades later retire at 45, then you can collect your retirement and do not have to wait until the rest of us do at 59.5. The only disadvantage is that your nest egg won't have the same benefit of the additional years of compound interest growth on the money that you take out of the account. The money that is left in there will indeed continue to grow and compound over time.

Now that was all a ton of information to digest. I hope it didn't exhaust you, but instead you are excited about what this all means for your future. The best retirement book that I have ever read that breaks this area all down specifically and succinctly in a non boring fashion is Chris Hogan's *Retire Inspired*. I highly suggest you pick up a copy and also log onto his site *chrishogan360.com* to utilize the retirement and investment tools that are free to help you with this process. In addition, he speaks about your RIQ, which stands for Retirement Intelligence Quotient, or the total amount that you will need to retire. This is great to understand based on your current lifestyle and how you desire to live out your retirement life in terms of how often you desire to travel, what you hope to do or give to others, etc. The nice thing is it gives us a baseline and we can figure out how much additionally we should invest based on the lifestyle we desire. Whether we decided to build our portfolio by utilizing our matching 401K plan or a Roth IRA, it is very important to know how your money is being invested.

How to Invest: Weighing Investment Volatility

The amount there is to include on how our retirement money is invested would fill countless books and a multitude of libraries. Depending upon who you speak to, opinions vary. However, a good rule of thumb to follow depends upon how much risk you are willing to take called volatility. You know how the saying goes, "The more risk, the more reward." This is exactly the case with our retirement accounts and portfolios. If we point the needle in the opposite direction and play things much too safe, we won't ever be able to fully retire. So for many folks, they will meet and settle on somewhere in the middle. Since the major point of a retirement account is indeed for just that, retirement, we have time to maximize compound interest and don't have to be overly aggressive. Taking the moderate approach is probably the best thing to do. When you are younger in your 20s and 30s it is appropriate to be a bit more aggressive and take more risks with the type of investments you are allocating your money towards. Once you get into your 40s, it is best to dial it back to mid level risk/tolerance ratio and then in your 50s to scale it back even further to less risky vehicles. Mitigating risk, especially toward the end of your working career is vital. If you do not and we have another crash like that of 2008 or the one we are just coming off of due to the COVID-19 Pandemic, you won't be retiring when expected and might have to work for an additional 3-4 years. We don't want that to happen. Although there are no guarantees, it is a pretty safe bet that if you follow this type of planning things will work out in your favor. For those who truly want to set it and forget it and are hands off types of investors, I suggest going with a LifeCycle fund. What this means is that your money for retirement is invested in a variety of different funds including stocks, bonds, mutual funds and more and will automatically lower your risk level over the decades, until the fund reaches completion. So a LifeCycle 2050 fund would be more risk oriented earlier on, while dialing way back over the final 5 or so years. For those of you who are more hands on and want to select the various funds you invest in based on what your employer's plan offers.

Specific Investment Options

The basic investment options include different size companies your money is invested with, as well as bonds, and a few other factors. Many people take a pizza pie approach toward allocating or distributing their invested dollars. Small cap funds are indeed just that, small companies that are worth less than $2billion dollars. Mid caps are those between $2 and $10 billion, while large cap funds are worth over $10 billion. Companies like Papa John's Pizza fall under the small cap section, an outfitter like American Eagle is a mid cap option, and the top dog's like Amazon, Facebook, and Apple make up the large cap type of companies. There are also a range of international companies as well. If you diversify and allocate between small, medium, and large caps at 25% a piece, mix in a 5-10% in international or emerging markets, and then another 5-10% in bonds, you will have a pretty nice mixture that will grow and not be too volatile. The best part is that you are not investing in a single stock, but it is a mutual fund approach, which below I will outline with more specificity. In short, mutual funds are a basket of 20-30 companies where you invest money in, I invest in, and Chloe invests in. Some of these will go up, while others might go down, but over the long haul more increase than decrease so your portfolio is on the rise over the long haul. If you invest in a single stock and have all of your eggs in one basket, if that stock does well, spectacular! If not, your entire investment can be destroyed! So mutual funds are the safest bet as it spreads your investment out like manure. Piled up in one area, manure stinks like crazy! Spread out, it is the miracle substance that crops need to grow and flourish. Mutual funds are more of the same. Remember that!

Other Vehicles: Stocks, Bonds, ETFs, Mutual Funds, Index Funds, and more

In this section we will discuss investment opportunities that fall outside of the strictly retirement realm. For a while I thought that I was set since I was working for a charter school that had a 6% employer investment match where I was fully vested from the get go. I contributed at least 6% from the start and by the time I left the company I had quite a substantial amount of over $100,000. However, I realized along the way that unless I planned on working until 59.5, which I absolutely do not, I had to do something more. I had to utilize another avenue with my investments. Not to mention, there were so many other vehicles on the lot so to speak in the investment world, that I didn't even realize were out there to drive. My suggestion is to at least go for a test drive in some of these areas or learn about them so that way when the time is right you can put some money into them. Diversifying your portfolio even more is important, as it will assist the growth of your net worth substantially.

Stocks

"The stock market is a device for transferring money from the impatient to the patient" -Warren Buffett

For most people who begin as investors, stocks are a scary vehicle. It is like jumping into a formula one race car that goes 0-60mph in a matter of a couple seconds. Stocks can be really great if you pick the right ones and really bad if you pool your money in a company that sinks. Stocks are beneficial overall when you spread your money amongst numerous companies and by paying attention to the market. Still, it isn't easy to continue to follow the trends or predict market swings which are bound to happen. We must do as best as we possibly can and tap into the sound advice of the pros. Of all investment vehicles, stocks are arguably the most volatile. The word stock, in the financial world, really means to literally "take hold of." In other words, when you invest in a stock or buy into a company, you own a portion of that company. That is what we call a share. You own a share or portion and are now a shareholder of the company which uses your money to continue to grow the business. In return they give you, the investor, money back in return in the form of dividends and interest. Again, when we invest in high quality stocks, we tend to make money at an average rate of 9.8% or so over the past 100 years. This is a pretty good rate of return if you ask me, while the bank only tends to yield 0.05% or so in interest. It all depends on the stock you decide to buy and how long you allow the money to exist in the market. Warren Buffet reminds us to be patient, as real gains take place over the long haul. Let's look at an example of how stocks work to understand this concept a bit further.

Chloe is doing well and has gotten a raise, she continues to maneuver her way through baby step four and her retirement account is on the rise. She desires to get into another vehicle and begins testing the stock world. She opens a single brokerage account which allows her to buy and sell stocks on her own. She could hire a financial advisor or overseer of her stock portfolio, which will minimally cost her 1-3% to tend to her funds. However, she has read this book and opens an account with Merrill Lynch, Fidelity, E-Trade, RobinHood or some other low cost brokerage. She should look at what fees each charges and after doing so she chooses Merrill Lynch, that is what I use, and now has a Merrill Edge Account to shop stocks. Chloe transfers $1,000 from the start and it goes into her Edge stock account. She knows that there are many large cap companies out there that seem tried and true like Apple, Disney, Microsoft, and others. She figures that since these companies have been around for a fairly long period of time and that they have gained in value over the long haul, these are a good way to start out. Chloe takes her $1,000 and buys three shares of Disney at $100 a share (total of $300), two shares of Apple at $275 per share ($550 total) and one share of Microsoft at $150. Chloe now is the owner of a piece of each of these three large cap companies. Her stock portfolio has been born. As each of the three stocks grow, her total investment grows accordingly. On the day she purchased Disney at $100 that was how much stake she put into the company per share for a total of $300 since she bought three shares. Let's say Disney is doing really well and in two months each share is worth $115. This means that her investment is now worth $115 per share or a total of $345. She made $45 over the past couple of months on her investment if she were to sell her shares. She can hold onto it or she can sell it. If she holds onto the Disney stock shares, there is a good possibility that it will continue to rise. However, it could drop in value. If it drops, then her investment will only be worth what each share of that stock is valued at according to what wall street deems the value is based on the market. Since the market ebbs and flows quite a bit, it's important to pay attention and be aware of what is happening with the stocks you hold. The reason why everyone, well many people that is, were freaking out during the Coronavirus pandemic from an investors standpoint is because the market dropped about 30%. Which, if we use the same example for Chloe would mean that her total $1,000 investment would be worth around $700 in value, costing her $300. This isn't that rough, but how about people who had $200,000 in stocks and they lost $60K. Yikes! The main thing to realize is that Chloe didn't actually lose anything yet, nor will you as an investor. On the flip side she didn't gain anything either when the stock shoots up in value. Nothing is lost or gained until one unloads and sells those shares of stock. Then and only then can we count it as a total gain or loss. On paper we can track stock gain or loss, but it is neither a true win or lose situation until the shares are actually sold. So what does that mean for you and for me? Well, the wise investor would understand that it is not a time to panic. Do not unload your stocks when the market is down. Instead, the time to sell is when the stock hits its peak. So how do you know that, there really is no great way to tell. Just make sure that when you sell the stock, if possible, that it is at a higher amount than when you purchased it so you make a profit. There are some cases where you might have to cut your losses when a stock continues to spiral downward. There are also technical ways to have stocks automatically sell if it is a certain amount or to buy them at a specific rate by putting stop quote limits and other technical attachments to them. We aren't going to get into those micro details here however.

The name of the stock game is that it's a really good vehicle, but it is volatile and risky. So you must be prepared for that. Who knows though, you might be investing in the next Amazon at $1.78 a share and it could turn into $2,000 per share over the course of a decade. Chances are that won't happen, but if you spread your stock investments out between some small cap, mid cap, and large cap companies, as well as across various sectors such as technology, health care, consumer goods and others in the market, you will win in the end. What about paying capital gains tax? Yes, there is money that you will have to pay on the gains you make on your stocks in the short term and long term, however there are ways to help shelter this somewhat. The nitty gritty isn't worth getting into at this point just yet, but you will see a table that shows the capital gains tax rates based on the dollar amount of your investments and gains. I want to paint a broad picture and give you an overall gist. Stocks like the other investment opportunities discussed in this section, outside of retirement funds, are accessible here in the now. This means when you invest money in them, there is no waiting years and years until you reach that magic number of 59.5! You can sell them whenever you desire within the 9:30-4pm eastern standard time frame, Monday-Friday. I have my favorite stock picks, but the main thing is that you do your research. Track the reports over the past year, five years, ten years, and longer to see the trend of the company and if it has linear progression over those courses of time. Try to invest in companies that you know about and also believe in. If the track record is positive on a company when you read up and the experts suggest this is something to invest in, go for it. You can always make changes. As long as your share holdings in those companies remain in the green, you are doing well. If they are red and going downward over an extended amount of time, especially outside of a recession, you might want to consider rebalancing your holdings.

Remember, when the market is down this for the wise investor means everything is on sale. A great time to buy more stocks is when the market dips because it will increase over father time! There is indeed a reason why Warren Buffet, one of the wealthiest men on the planet, has done so well in the stock market. The answer is time. Over the course of time and riding the up and down roller coaster waves of the stock exchange, it will indeed rise. Be patient and heed the advice of those who have had great success before. This not only applies to stocks, but to all investments. Time is on our side and must be utilized to materialize wealth. Net worth is not about today and today only, but all investments compiled over the course of one's lifetime. I suggest an overall in depth analysis done to your stock portfolio at least once a year with quarterly check ins along the way. Personally, I like to track things on my phone daily, but if you get too caught up in it, you might drive yourself crazy as it is a roller coaster type of ride. For those of you out there who are really looking forward to building a sizable investment portfolio through stocks, I suggest subscribing to a service such as *The Motley Fool*. When I began putting money into the stock market, I signed up for a year subscription to *The Motley Fool* where I received daily emails, could tune into webinars, as well as in depth analysis on stocks that I held from the experts Tom and David Gardener. The cost of such a subscription tends to run around $10 a month. For me it was a great way to learn the ins and outs, become well versed and maximize my gains. In addition, this is a whole lot cheaper than hiring a fund manager.

2020 Tax Rates on Long Term Capital Gains

	For Unmarried Individuals	For Married Individuals Filing Joint Returns	For Heads of Households
	Taxable Income Over		
0%	$0	$0	$0
15%	$40,000	$80,000	$53,600
20%	$441,450	$496,600	$469,050
	Additional Net Investment Income Tax		
3.8%	MAGI above $200,000	MAGI above $250,000	MAGI above $200,000

Source: "2020 Tax Brackets," Tax Foundation and IRS Topic Number 559

ETFs

Yet another viable vehicle to drive off the lot when you are investing and trying to accumulate a higher net worth includes ETFs. ETFs are what are known as Exchange Traded Funds. By definition, they are an investment fund traded on stock exchanges, similar to stocks, but with some other benefits. An ETF holds assets such as stocks, commodities, or bonds and generally operates with an arbitrage mechanism designed to keep it trading close to its net asset value, although deviations can occasionally occur. What this means is that an ETF is composed of a variety of investments compiled together including numerous companies and has a greater likelihood of increasing or at least is less volatile. As opposed to the single stock, which is partial ownership of one company, the ETF is a fund that spreads the money out between numerous areas. However, it can still be traded on the spot like a stock can. Personally, I am a big fan of ETFs. Especially when we can purchase them in various sectors. For example a great cloud computing technology ETF in 2020 has been SKYY. A number of companies are included in this ETF such as Amazon, Microsoft, Oracle, Alphabet, Alibaba, and more. The ETF is very similar to what we will discuss next, mutual funds.

Mutual Funds

Most 401K plans, 403(b)s, ETFs, index funds and others are made up of an arrangement of mutual funds. We discussed this a bit earlier, but let's dig a little deeper into the benefits of the mutual fund. A mutual fund is literally a fund, mutually owned by a multitude of people. Similar to a stock offered by a company is owned share by share by thousands of investors, the greater benefit of the mutual fund is that it involves many companies under one roof so to speak. If you are investing in a technology based mutual fund family then you will be pooling the money you choose to invest in 20 or so companies in this sector. For example, Chloe decides that she wants to invest her next $1,000 in a tech based mutual fund and goes with Red Oak Technology Select Fund (ROGSX). Within this mutual fund family there exists top dogs like Google, Apple, Microsoft, Cisco Systems, Facebook, and others including companies like Intel and more. The great thing is that her $1,000 is spread out amongst these companies at the percentage rate the fund is set at. This has a two-fold meaning. First, each company within the mutual fund has a certain percentage that every dollar she invests is allocated toward. Second, if Apple as a company goes up in value and stock share holds increase and Microsoft decreases in value, Chloe can still make gains on her mutual fund investment. This option is the most popular one by many investors who want to mitigate risk and still make adequate gains to build wealth. You can invest in mutual funds outside of retirement plans and I suggest you do so, as this money is liquid. What this means is that you can have access to it whenever you desire by selling off the value of the fund and acquiring the cash for what it is worth.

Index Funds

The newest trend to invest in is the index fund route. According to *Investopedia*, an index fund by definition is *a type of mutual fund with a portfolio constructed to match or track the components of a financial market index, such as the S&P's 500 Index. An index mutual fund is said to provide broad market exposure, low operating expenses and low portfolio turnover.* The index fund is fairly similar to the mutual fund, but it is more closely aligned to the index, hence the name. The best index fund families to invest in, which I have chosen to take advantage of over the past few years and will continue to do so, include those offered by Vanguard. So why put money into index funds opposed to traditional mutual funds? Well, the cost expense ratio is lower with index funds. Most mutual fund holdings charge at least a set 1%. So what an investor actually sees as their interest rate of return for a mutual fund, is actually lower than what you truly gained. This is due to the percentage it costs for the holding company to run the fund. In layman's terms this means that if Chloe gains 10% in her tech based mutual fund, then she most likely acquired a true rate of 11% in gains over that time period, the difference paying for the fund maintenance. Meanwhile, an index fund charges only a fraction of a percent in most cases, meaning more money in Chloe's pocket for net return since the cost expense ratio is significantly lower.

Recommendations

I am a total fan of the following Vanguard index funds and ETFs: Vanguard Information Technology (VGT), VANGUARD IX FUN/S&P 500 ETF (VOO), Vanguard Mid-Cap ETF (VO), Vanguard Small Cap (VB), Vanguard Health Care ETF (VHT), Vanguard FTSE Developed (VEA). Personally, I have invested over $100,000 spread across these index funds and ETFs, which are yielding anywhere from 8-12% or more in interest dividends on average per year.

Bonds

When I hear the word bond, I automatically think of 007 and the man, the myth, the legend, James Bond. The thrilling movies that kept me glued to the edge of my seat with high drama and crazy excitement, rush into the picture. Although these cinematic gems kept movie goers watching avidly for years, bonds in the financial world are the exact opposite. They are anything but exciting. Bonds are not the flash in the pan, one hit wonders that stocks can be. They tend to be much more steady and far less volatile over time. Some people would even argue that bonds are straight boring. Bonds do help to bulletproof your investment portfolio and should make up anywhere between 8-12% of your total investments.   Since bonds are not very volatile, their interest yield tends to be significantly lower than stocks or most index funds as well. Although long term government bonds over the past 100 years have gone up by about 5%, which is about half of the S&P 500's rate, they are a much safer option. For many bonds though, there is often a specific time length that your money has to be in the fund account for, before you can access it. There are accounts such as non qualified bond funds that I have invested in over the years, that allow you to have access to your money at any time. The only caveat is, you can get your money as long as you pay an upfront fee percentage or a very low withdrawal percentage on the money you take out. You have the choice. The expense to do so by no means significant at all. Long story short, bonds are a great way to grow your portfolio over the long haul, while diverting risk. Typically bonds ride the opposite wave of stocks, meaning that when the market is hot and stocks are on the rise (BULL Market), bonds are falling. When the market dips and turns downward (Bear Market), then the value of bonds increases. So playing them off of one another can help, especially investing in 10% or so bonds because they will almost always increase an adequate and steady amount over time. There are a ton of different kinds of bonds and you can invest in companies that utilize bonds to expand and grow, as they are connected to this realm. Additionally, there are government bonds and probably the most commonly known type, savings bonds. Just know that this is not the sports car of investment vehicles, by any means.   I liken bonds to old faithful and steady Eddy. They are the Chevy Malibu of the vehicle class if you will. Bonds will help get you there safely over the course of time.

Compound Interest

One of the smartest guys of all time, Albert Einstein was enamored with the concept of compound interest. I didn't quite realize this "8th wonder of the world," until I fully took advantage of loading up my retirement and investment accounts. Compound interest *aka* the formula of all formulas: $A = P(1+r/n)^{nt}$. Come on, you don't know that one? Haha, neither did I. The nice thing is we don't have to be a math wizard to figure it out. What Mr. Einstein and other great science and math geniuses realized is that compound interest boils down to the additional interest added to the principal (original amount) and sum of a deposit. Even more simply put, interest on top of interest. It comes as a result of reinvesting the interest each time it is earned, as opposed to getting a payout for it. This in essence is where the compounding happens and exponential growth occurs. The best part here is that we are not talking about bamboo in a jungle! We are talking about that other green, namely money!

Example of the Magic Known as Compound Interest

Chloe is doing well with her investments. She is now earning compound interest on the money she continues to put into her 401K as well as on her stock holdings, tech mutual fund accounts, and index funds. Fast forward a few years and her total amount in her 401K has grown to $50,000. The good news is that the market is doing really well and yielding a 15% return. Her $50,000 is up 15% and is now worth $57,500. The following year she added that same $8,000 total contribution coming from her $54,600 salary (9%+employer match of 6%) and she has $65,500 in her retirement account. But wait, there is more! Her investment continues to compound at another 12% meaning that she just made interest on that interest and Chloe actually has a grand total of $73,360. Dan, I am liking this! You and me both! The best and most alarming example I ever heard with regard to compound interest that put it's growth magnitude in perspective for me is the one I am going to share with you now. Say you took a $1,000, the same amount we had you save up for your initial baby step one to start out. You put that $1K away in an index fund or another mutual fund account, 401K or IRA and it grows at an average rate of 9%. You do not add a single dollar to it over the next 40 years. You would have a few thousand dollars right? Wrong! Even if that were true, that would be far better than the couple bucks you would have made by putting it in a traditional savings account in the bank. I mean, how much could the total possibly be as nothing was added to the initial investment. Take a guess at how much you think it could be worth. Well, the $1,000 after year one of gaining 9% interest would be worth $1,090. Come on, only a $90 increase? Remember, don't worry, we are working with bamboo here. After year two, that $1,090 compounds at 9% again and is now worth $1,188.10. By year three it is worth $1,295.03. Fast forward to year 10, that initial $1,000 has more than doubled and is worth $2,367.36. After year 20 it has a value of $5,604.41, more than five times the original amount you started with. So you are probably thinking okay well it will be worth a few thousand more by year 30. This is the part that starts to really excite me. Your investment more than doubles again over the next decade and is worth $13,267.28. But we are still not done yet. The craziest part is that the next ten years are the most significant of them all as the concept of time has really played into this equation. By year 40, your $1,000 initial investment, without adding a penny to the principal, has compounded at an annual rate of 9% to reach a total sum and exorbitant value of $31,409.42. Wholly smokes! That is wild shiz. You have more than 30X your initial investment. Can you see the power of compounding now? And that was only with $1,000. What if you were able to invest $6,000 per year for forty years? What if I told you that by doing so at that same rate of return of 9% (which is lower than the S&P by nearly an entire percentage point over the past century) your total dollar amount you would have invested would have been $240,000. That is a nice chunk of change to put in. However, that initial investment pales in comparison to the mammoth nest egg pile of $2,400,000 you are able to sit on! I might as well call you a multi-millionaire. This is very possible for you, but you have to get in the game!

The Rule of 72

Berkshire Hathaway Hedge Fund, which has made Warren Buffet one of the world's wealthiest people, might not be touchable for us in terms of making millions or even billions of dollars. Unless of course you buy in via the stock exchange and purchase single shares of this conglomerate. However, we can still exercise the same principals on a micro scale that Buffet has taken full advantage of throughout the years and have our own success. After studying many great investors and reading a multitude of literature, all of which I will share with you in the final sections of this book, it is essential to follow keen advice. The seasoned veterans that are tried and true should be our go to for an impactful blueprint in the realm of finance. What I like most about Buffet is that he is very humble, still living on a meagre budget as he resides in his house from 1958. The billionaire sticks to a routine by getting a $3 egg sandwich breakfast daily from the McDonald's drive through, where he pulls up with his $50,000 modest Cadillac. I can relate to this, besides for being a fast food junkie that is. Regardless of your taste in food, or the car you drive, this picture is similar to my own and that is what makes it relevant. Being an educator myself, I certainly understand and stress the fact that knowledge is power. So when Warren Buffet says that the book *The Intelligent Investor* by Benjamin Graham is his financial bible, you better believe that I sure as heck own a copy of it and have read it cover to cover. For the newer investor this resource can be a little heavy in terms of the material content. However, what I want to highlight now in this section, is one of the biggest takeaways from the text that will help us comprehend the magnitude of compound interest and give us a way to compute predictions.

So what is the big takeaway or top secret you might be wondering? Well, it is the *rule of 72*. Now you don't have to be a mathematician to understand this one and it breaks down fairly easily. The *rule of 72* will help you and I better realize the power of our investment growing each year and be able to make accurate projections to what our financial portfolio or scope will look like based on the amount of interest we are earning. This is an infallible formula and is something I had to share. So let's get started with this exciting formula! The *rule of 72* is all about figuring out how long it will take for our money to double. Now we are all familiar with the phrase, *double or nothing*. Lots of risk, chance, and luck is involved in gambling and putting our odds down to that type of situation. The best part of the *rule of 72* is that it is all double, and it eliminates the nothing part of the saying. How the *rule of 72* works is it allows the investor, like you or me, to compute the number of years required to double one's money based on a given interest rate. The exact science behind it is as follows: **Divide the interest rate into 72.** Wait, that's it? Yes, it is that simple and easy. For example, if you want to know how long it would take to double your money at nine percent interest, simply divide 9 into 72 and get 8 years. Let's bring back Chloe into the equation for a moment to see how this might work for her and some of the investments she has been making.

Chloe continues to work hard at XCompany. She is doing so well that they have awarded her a promotion. With that new position, along with many other great benefits in being a leader now for her firm, she has earned a significant bump in pay. As we mentioned previously and that which cannot be overstated, income is the greatest and most powerful wealth building tool. How Chloe utilizes this large change in salary is the key. Now, she has become wise over the years and is disciplined. We will unpack standard of living later on, but for now I want to focus on the *rule of 72*. Using her increased money each month, Chloe sat down and was crunching some numbers. The good news at this point is that her retirement portfolio is now worth over $100,000 and continues to climb, meanwhile she has another $30,000 in a mixture of stocks, mutual funds, index funds, and bonds, as well as owning a rental property. Needless to say, well into baby step four, Chloe is doing really well. Chloe is interested in finding out how long it will take for her money to double. Now remember that this is a projective measure and not an absolute guarantee. Since the stock market will continue to ebb and flow and the real estate market fluctuate some, there are factors that cannot be 100% accurate when making a prediction. After all, that is why we call it a prediction. Yet, the *rule of 72* works every time and is accurate with regard to making a prediction.   In any event, Chloe sits down and after analyzing her retirement gains over the past few years, she does a similar data dive by pouring over the reports to see how her stock holdings and other investment funds have been doing. She sees that she has been averaging about a 10% return over the past five years across the board, besides for bonds which have yielded 4.9%. This is super! Chloe has learned to educate herself well, make smart decisions, hope for the best, and also be prepared for any lulls in the market. Therefore, when she computes her finances by utilizing the *rule of 72* to predict the next doubling of her money, she will use a more modest 8% interest rate to calculate how long it will take for her various accounts to double in size! Her accounts might double sooner, but she wants to be on the safe side of planning out her life. Chloe begins with the $100,000 she has in her retirement. Chloe takes 8% and divides that into 72 and gets 9 (72/8=9). So it will take her approximately nine years for her retirement portfolio to reach $200,000. She can apply the same simplistic math for the other accounts. However, this is only if she does not add anything additionally to her retirement or other investments. If she continues to contribute the 9% plus the 6% employer match to her 401K for example, this will accelerate the process for her to be able to double her money. Even when using a very safe investment vehicle such as a bond, it is nice to know that at 5% interest it would take about 14 or so years to double one's money. Personally, I like playing with the numbers and making some projections. In the appendix section of this text I have included a number of great resources. One is an outline of how much one should try to have invested in retirement by certain ages to be on track to end the work phase around time of collection. For those of you like me, who wish to stop working sooner, we will have some more to discuss in the coming chapters on achieving financial independence. Not only are making projections fun to do, they help us stay on course and understand the power of building wealth. Investing is the area in your finances that will ultimately allow us to have an even more choice filled life.

So why don't more people resort to wise investments that take full advantage of compound interest or the *rule of 72*? Well, they are in debt for starters, are undisciplined, or simply do not realize what their money can do for them if put into the right vehicles. If you are like me and want to live comfortably later on and have that dream retirement, let alone be able to stop working by gaining financial freedom and independence years and years before the average person, keep reading and keep investing. No matter what age you are or where you are today, your investments will help you paint a much brighter and more affluent future. Your future self will be so happy that you did. And for those young bucks out there who are just starting out, make this a habit from the very beginning. You won't even realize the difference of $125 or even $200 from your paycheck if it is what you already had done for years. Doing so will allow you to sit on a pile of money that grows on it's own without you doing anything differently. All you have to do is keep working and do what you are already doing. Minimize any stupid purchases or negative debt and you will become a champion of finance. But at this stage in the game, I don't have to worry about you being dumb with your money as you have established the habits of a disciplined winner.

The easiest compound interest calculator that I have found and use on a regular basis is the one accessible online on *Money Chimp*. Use it and run the numbers. It is a fun way to get excited about your investments and the factor of compound interest. For those people you care about and whose futures you wish to see as bright as yours will now be, share this information with them.

http://www.moneychimp.com/calculator/compound_interest_calculator.htm

CHALLENGE # 5: *Invest 15% of your money in a retirement fund.*

Once you hit baby step four, contact your HR rep and find out if your employer offers a match, pension plan, or some other retirement opportunity. If they do, by all means, take the free money and at least begin by investing the minimum to get the match. Personally, I would utilize the match as soon as you can even if you aren't at baby step four yet because you don't want to miss out on the free money. Not to mention, compound interest works best when started early and can have the most time to mature and grow. Eventually, build this retirement contribution amount up to 15% of your take home pay and watch your investment blossom over time.

CHALLENGE # 6: *Invest extra money in stocks, index funds, or non retirement accounts.*

Once you have 15% invested in your retirement account and you have some more money coming in, instead of wasting it away on things you won't remember in twenty years let alone a year from now, open up a brokerage account. Start investing in stocks, index funds or bond options. Heck, do all three! Watch your net worth be on the rise. Remember, this money will be accessible to you whenever you desire to utilize it. The money in these investments is liquid and could be put toward that next car you wish to buy in cash, the down payment on that next home or rental property, as well as any other expenses you have. It will yield a far greater return than any bank savings account out there.

"Real estate cannot be lost or stolen, nor can it be carried away. Purchased with common sense, paid for in full, and managed with reasonable care, it is about the safest investment in the world."

-Franklin D. Roosevelt

CHAPTER 8: Real Estate

"Landlords grow rich in their sleep." -John Stuart Mill

A new area that I have gotten into lately has been the world of real estate. What many people do not realize is that real estate has much more to do than the very four walls that you live within on a daily basis. 90% of the world's wealthiest individuals have implemented real estate investments and built a sizable portfolio. I am very excited for us to discuss this realm and to share with you some avenues that are out there. Real estate has been up over 11% over the past twenty years and the best part is that it can have even higher yields based on market trends. The volatility factor is half that of stocks, which is huge. Even during the 2008 crash when the S&P fell 37%, the real estate market only dropped 6.7%. Commercial real estate is where the big money is at being up over 430% throughout the past 20 years. However, most investors reading this text don't have tens of thousands of dollars at a clip or more to pump into big builds going on in the commercial world. Therefore, we will focus primarily on residential real estate. If you desire to take a stake in commercial real estate and don't have the sizable capital that is required or are not an accredited lender, you can buy real estate ETFs and stock holdings in this realm. I have done so and they can be very profitable over the long haul. Take REITS such as STAG for example, you can buy into this commercial real estate company for as little as $25 a share (as of 2020) or Realty Income Corporation (O) which is a trust that invests in single tenant commercial properties in the U.S., Puerto Rico, and the United Kingdom ($50 a share as of April 2020).

Why Real Estate is a Solid Investment & Configuring ROI

Real estate is such a profitable investment option because it allows us as investors to essentially have a tenant, the one renting the property, to pay for the mortgage. Meanwhile, you gain wealth and some extra cash flow during the process by mostly sitting back and enjoying the ride. This is really good and what we call passive income. Whenever we can have another person or a few people pay for an investment and reap the rewards, that is ideal. I suggest you pick up a copy of the *The Book on Rental Property Investing: How to create wealth and passive income through smart buy and hold real estate investing* by

Brandon Turner. This one will get into all of the ins and outs of the rental property game with great specificity and depth. For now, I will highlight some of the key components of the benefits to investing in a rental property and how to build net worth while doing so.

One of the main reasons why buying another property is smart, if you already have a home, is to maximize the equity. Simply put, when it comes to real estate, equity can be explained as the difference between the fair market value of the property and the amount of money a person owes on the mortgage. In order to figure out the calculation for real estate equity this can be done so by deducting the mortgage value from the fair market value of the property. For example, when Chloe is ready to purchase her next home as an investment property, she browses the market and does some assessments. She sees a nice duplex that is in a great area within a high rent district in Cleveland, Ohio and ends up purchasing it for $200,000. The mortgage on this rental home including taxes, after she put 20% down, comes in at $1,250 per month. Since Chloe has paid down 20% of the purchase price, she has $40,000 or so in equity in her home, less closing costs ($200,000 house value - down payment=total equity). This means she owns a fifth of the house outright. The great news is unlike a typical mortgage where one is living in the home and paying it off on their own, since it is a rental property and Chloe has two tenants, those renters are the one's footing the bill. Chloe's $1,250 rental property costs her nothing at all outside of the money she laid out initially for the down payment. She set her rent for each side of the duplex at $1,150 per month, a common amount for this area and a fair ask for the property she holds. Therefore, Chloe has $2,300 coming in each month. After paying the $1,250 to the mortgage company, she nets $1,050. There are some things she has to consider such as property tax (in this case it was escrowed or built into the mortgage, homeowners insurance for the property, utilities (built into the rent cost-have the renters pay this), upkeep, vacancy possibilities, expenses for repairs, water, sewer, gas, and snow/lawn care. When you combine all of these with the cost of the mortgage you get what is called your total monthly expense on the property. After subtracting your total monthly expenses from the income she brought in for the month on the rent, Chloe has her monthly cash flow amount. Cash flow equates to how much she actually earned on the rental property during the month. In the real estate world, the profit earned is referred to as ROI (Return On Investment). To calculate your ROI (interest % you gained on the property), you need to take the total investment (how much you put into the property initially-for Chloe that was $40,000) and divide the cash flow amount X12 because that is how much cash flow one would receive for a year. That would then give you the rate of return on the investment or ROI.

So let's say Chloe's cash flow was $450 per month ($450X12=$5,400). She invested $40,000 initially, so we have to take those figures to compute her ROI which is as follows: ($5,400/$4000=0.135) or a 13.5% ROI. Now this is clearly a great investment. Chloe's home is earning her a much higher rate than the stock market average of 9.8% and in the meantime, the value of the property she holds continues to climb. Within ten years of continuing to collect her rent from the tenants, as well as paying down the loan simultaneously, Chloe's equity margin will increase vastly. Her property is now worth an additional $30,000. She has paid down her loan (really her tenants have) by over $60,000, so she now has over an $80,000 stake in the home. Meanwhile the rental property is worth over $230,000. If she were to sell it today, she would be making that 13.5% gain on top of the increase in the property value, less taxes for capital gains (15-20% rate). However, there is a way to avoid paying these capital gains taxes by filing a *1031 Exchange*. According to the IRA, a *1031* allows you to legally bypass paying capital gains taxes when you sell an investment property and reinvest the proceeds from the sale within certain time limits in a property or properties of a like kind that are of equal or greater value. In other words, if you use the real estate money earned to invest in another property, you avoid getting banged up with a 15-20% tax bill from Uncle Sam. This is huge because losing that amount would significantly hurt your overall investment gain. This is largely why once people enter the real estate market as an investor, they stay in the game because the profits are there to be built upon. Once a given property is paid off fully, the investor then will be piling up cash flow in the thousands per month on a duplex property that is costing them very minimal amounts to maintain. If one were to have multiple properties, even better. But for now starting with one duplex for Chloe is a good way to enter the real estate market.

Navigating Property Maintenance & what it takes to be a Real Estate Investor

Well, what if I am not handy at all and do not want to deal with tenants waking me up in the middle of the night to change a damn lightbulb? Good news is, the light bulb can wait, after all it's night time! With all seriousness however, being bombarded by a tenant is a legitimate concern. It is a valid point to be made.

Unfortunately, if you have a problem with this then real estate is not for you. Sorry. No, I am just kidding! This is the farthest thing from the truth. You nor Chloe doesn't have to have a degree in construction management. Whether she can swing a hammer well or not doesn't really matter. No problem at all. Don't worry. Tune into some Bob Marley and listen to the calming words, "Every little thing is gonna be alright." Many people hire property managers for around $200 a month. The property manager will take care of all the rent collections, repairs, complaints by tenants, and whatever else you delegate for them to do as part of their job you pay them for. Or you can do it on your own if you are handy and willing to take care of the organizational pieces. That is up to you to decide. Everything has a worth. If you have a couple of properties, the fee for property management will be a little higher, but it becomes of greater value as this jack of all trades (property manager) will save you a ton of time. They will also eliminate any headaches, since that is their job.

Big Money is in Real Estate

Real estate is a lucrative asset in the medium and long run for a number of reasons. First, it is always a sought after commodity. Let's face it, people need a place to go home to and businesses (commercial real estate) have to have a place to do their work. It is what we call a finite good with a limited supply as there is only so much land to build upon in valuable areas or places where people desire to live. That is why finding a hot rental district is key. So do your homework and work with a realtor to find this out and you will be happy you did. Second, zoning laws limit the amount of construction that is allowed in a given area. Third, real estate offers depreciation tax shields, while appreciating in value. Fourth, that *1031 Exchange* helps to defer the capital gains tax for years so that way the value of the investment grows and compounds without costing the investor a ton of money. Lastly, there is leverage with real estate that enhances the overall returns. If I haven't convinced you yet as to why real estate is a great vehicle for investment, I might never do so.

The more I learned about real estate the more I knew that I had to get in on this part of the financial game. Remember, 90% of the world's wealthiest people own real estate. And in a market that has over $200 trillion in it, I am liking our chances in doing well over time. There will always be business and you can be certain that if you plan it out and acquire a property in a growing location or popular rent district you will increase your growth potential significantly. Think about it, if over the next decade you acquired another property every couple of years, you would have five or so properties. If each got around the same ROI as Chloe's or even a little less, you would have built a serious stock pile in the rental property game. Possibly, this could be enough to allow you to be financially independent to the point where you no longer needed to work that 9-5 job, but instead can go part time at a place you desire. Over time, as those properties become paid off, you no longer have to work at all and will have another big pile of cash accumulating monthly because of your rental incomes. If you wanted to sell the properties off for a lump sum payment and are okay with paying the capital gains tax, you could reinvest those lump sums in index funds and almost gain back what you initially lost in the taxation. The options with this sector are vast.

The final area of real estate that I would like to accentuate and shed light on is storage. Over the course of time, everyone acquires a ton of stuff. We are driven by a materialistic society. People are radical consumers and constantly buying more and more. The thing about it is, rarely are they purging all of these things, but collection and hoarding seems to be more of the norm. Burying these items in the basement of the house is one thing, but for those who live in cities across America and areas where there is far less space due to supply and demand, storage units are often a must. As a result, I highly suggest getting acclimated with this side of real estate. Purchasing a larger building or buying a plot of land and putting up some cheap, yet durable construction to create a storage center is a huge way to gain money each month and maximize passive income. These units are very easy to maintain or manage because essentially the tenant is putting their belongings in there and it is secure, being accessible to the person renting the unit only. Seasonal visits by tenants to a storage unit is more par for the course. The amount of traffic one would have or the time it would require to manage on one's own is fairly minimal. You can set these up any way you would like, charge a variety of prices based on the size of the units you offer, and have many tenants footing the bill monthly. I see a lot of green coming your way down the pipeline if you are feeling good about this avenue of real estate.

Real Estate as a Bullet Proof Investment

Real estate is as bullet-proof of an investment as bullet-proof gets! Don't get me wrong, there are some bad properties in locations that we should stay away from. It is crucial as mentioned before to do our homework and know what we are getting into. Not every deal out there is a good deal. However, if you utilize the strategies and tips that have been outlined, shop around, and really consider this as a viable and feasible option, you can become a property owner. The old phrase *landlord* might not be used as much anymore, but over the course of centuries the people who have always held the highest stakes in society were the ones who controlled the land. After all, like him or not, that is what Christopher Columbus and the other explorers did when they came to our country and started out. As populations are on the rise and the life expectancy continues to increase, land and property ownership becomes even more valuable. As Roosevelt said, "You cannot steal someone's home, or carry away their place of residence." I believe that it is time for the wise investor, which you are becoming, to add that duplex or even a single family home to your repertoire. As long as there is a tenant living inside, you are making a lot of money. And even during a brief vacancy period, you are building equity by paying down the loan.

Before moving on to the next topic of discussion, I wanted to take a moment to unveil some of the exact math that comes along with being a rental home owner and utilizing it as an investment. Many of these principles can be applied to your own home which you reside in as well. In a later chapter, we will examine a deep data dive I conducted. One of the many people I interviewed and collected qualitative and quantitative data from was Sarah, a married mother of two. She had this to say about her home, "I wish I knew sooner to buy a house because renting was just handing over my money to someone else." Sarah's insight is correct and the math below when it comes to building equity on the investment of a house is quite impressive.

Real Estate Value Increases Over Time

In ten years a $200,000 property that was purchased will be worth around $230,000 thanks to the value of the home increasing as the market continues to rise. By renting this property out, the tenants will have paid your mortgage down by at least $40,000. That initial loan that you took out after a 20% down payment was $160,000, is now down to $120,000. Meanwhile, you will have made $12,600 in rent per year, less upkeep and a property manager fees, vacancy costs, and other expenses. Factoring in repairs and total costs, in many instances you will net $7,000 each year as a profit on top of the mortgage being paid in full by the tenants. Having done so for the past decade, now being ten years down the road, this is a total of $70,000 more in your pocket. When combined with the equity and increased value in the home, as well as paying down your $1,250 monthly mortgage (done so by the tenants remember) you will have made nearly $100,000 on the property. If you or I were to repeat this process for a few properties, we could accumulate wealth very quickly. I hope you now can see a bit more clearly how and why real estate is the area where the rich get richer. The graphic below shows the spread between appreciation and the loan being paid down, which is essentially the amount of equity accrued (money you have in your home as far as worth).

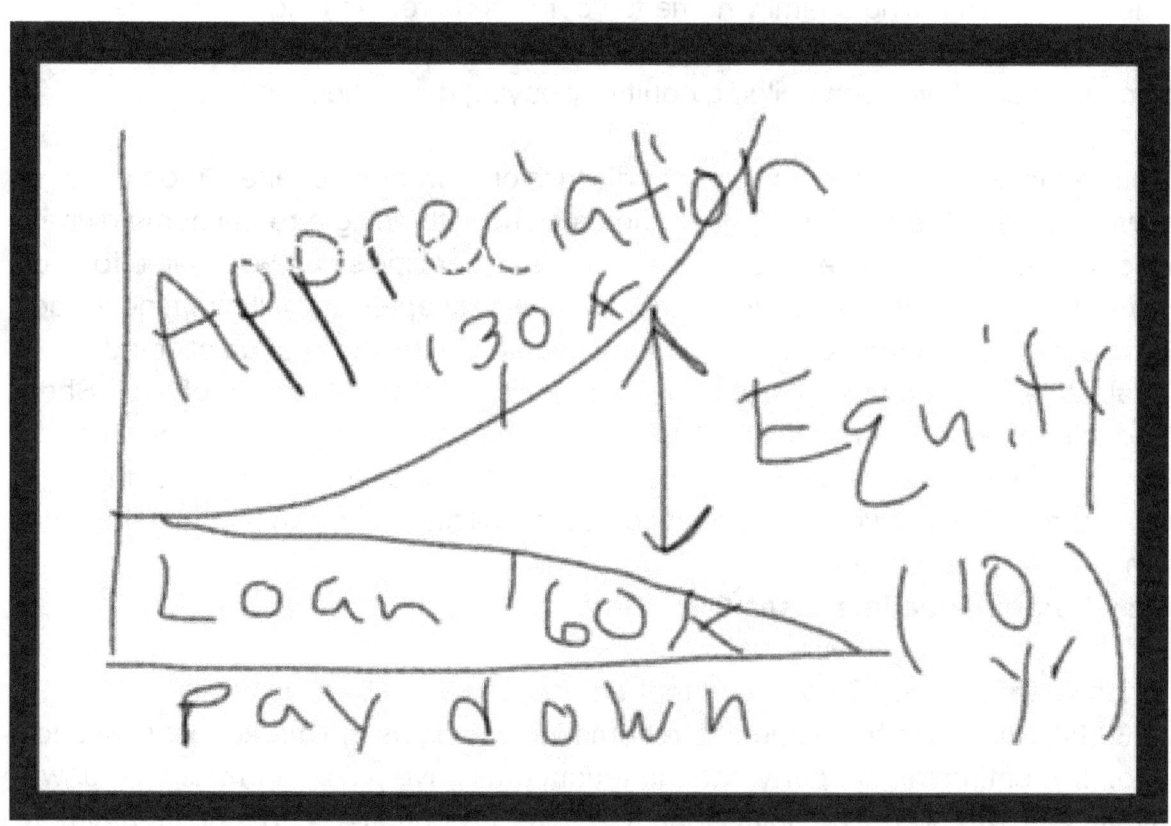

Overall, there is a ton to learn about this sector of investing. Read up and learn all that you can. Get into your first rental property and if you can, make it a duplex or triplex. Utilize house hacking, as you split up the house into sections and each tenant pays rent. Hire a property manager if you desire to not have to do anything at all, except oversee the funding. Be willing to hold onto the property for the long haul and maximize the ROI. Increase equity and build your net worth. Before you know it, you will be living out a real live game of *Monopoly*. Like that funny little man with the white mustache and top hat, you too will be smiling all the way to the bank. The best part will be that it is on someone else's dime. Make sure to get in on this financial vehicle. I would much rather see you being the landlord than the one renting. It is my hope that you are the one making the real money that is out there for the taking. I am excited to join you in buying my next property as soon as possible because the proof is in the pudding, and this one is rich to the taste.

CHALLENGE #7: When you get to baby step 4 & beyond save to buy real estate.

For many of you, this challenge might not be applicable for a number of years, but that is okay. Put it on the back burner, just remember to leave the stove on. Real estate is a big avenue that must be taken advantage of. Even if you purchase just one extra property you will be accelerating your net worth growth by years and also adding to that nest egg down the line. Thousands of people who have literally no carpentry skills and are certainly not realtors are taking full advantage of the $200 trillion that is out there to capitalize on. Maybe we will never own something as large and spectacular as a Marriott beach front hotel in Maui, but having a rental property or two will add great value to an already robust asset class that you have worked hard for and stacked your ever growing portfolio with. Turn the key on real estate and open a door that will make the housing market make you wealthy for years to come!

"The Key to a lifestyle of freedom is to create passive income."

-Mike Wolf

CHAPTER 9: Passive Income

I looked at the clock and it was certainly time to go to bed. We had a big day ahead of us tomorrow, as we would be on the road to celebrate Christmas down state with my family. Regardless of the situation of the next day to come, we all need sleep to recharge and rejuvenate ourselves. I began to think about one of my favorite stories I had read to my nephew and niece over the past month or so, *The Night Before Christmas.* You know how the line goes…"The children were nestled all snug in their beds, while visions of sugar plums danced in their heads." Now, you might be thinking to yourself, what the heck does this have to do with my finances or gaining financial freedom? Well, unlike the children who had visions of sugar plums on this particular night, I continue to have other visions dancing in my head. The best part of it is that it is not on one night a year in the hopes that "St. Nick would soon be there!" My bed time visions and story go more like this… "Dan jumped into his warm cozy bed, while visions of dollar bills danced again in his head." Yes, dollar bills are dancing in my mind and the greatest part is it is not a dream, it is a reality. You don't have to be obsessed with making money and have it always on your mind. What I will talk about next is utilizing multiple passive income streams.

Benefits of Passive Income

Passive income is arguably the ninth wonder of the world. What is better than literally making money in our sleep! By definition, passive income involves earnings derived from an investment or revenue stream in which a person is not actively involved in. To boil it down, passive income is earning money which happens on its own without our time or effort. When passive income is continuously reoccurring, it is known as residual income, as it comes to the investor each month. I cannot speak for everyone out there, but most of us work hard on a weekly basis to earn a salary or hourly wage that keeps our house afloat, puts food on the table, and provides us opportunities to become an investor. It is time for us to start, if we haven't done so already, to truly take what is out there and make it work for us. The various investment vehicles that we have covered up to this point all fall under the umbrella of passive income. Inevitably there are some that are greater sources of passive income than others. Warren Buffet said it best, "If you don't find a way to make money while you sleep, you will work until you die." I don't want to have to keep working and life is too short to be consumed by our jobs. Money will always be necessary, but how we make that money is the differentiating factor that will change our lives either for better or worse.

Passive income allows us to grow our wallet, net worth, and overall financial stockpile quickly. When we put our money in the right places we can have in many cases a second salary coming in on a regular basis. Take a moment to imagine what your life could be like if you had another $1,000 coming your way each month. What would you do differently? How would this eliminate stress? What experiences would you and your family be able to afford to do? All of this is important to dream about because it is time to make it a reality. See, the best part of the human mind and capacity is that thought is the first step that leads to action. For many of us, and I fell into this category previously, we must unshackle our minds. We have unfortunately chained our brains and put a governor on our mindsets. We are too limited with our thoughts. Our ability to think outside of the box when it comes to many things has been suppressed. This is often the case with regard to our finances. Doing something different is the only way to initiate change. Like all change, it does involve some risk and perhaps some uncomfortable moments. Sacrifice isn't easy. Being disciplined from the start is not desired by most, but the outcome and finish line is what we are aiming for are we not? No, I am not talking about having to wait years and years to reap the reward. When it comes to passive income, it is all about the here and the now. Oh yeah, and passive income will take care of us in the future too! So what are we waiting for? Let's get this passive income party started.

Different Types of Passive Income

This is what expert investor and money man Steve Fisher had to say about passive income, "Residual income is passive income that comes in every month whether you show up or not. It's when you no longer get paid on your personal efforts alone, but you get paid on the efforts of hundreds or even thousands of others and on the efforts of your money! It's one of the keys to financial freedom and time freedom." What this statement by Fisher has explained and taught me is profound. I believe what he is getting at is that no matter how hard of a worker you are, no matter how creative, innovative or talented you may be, there is no replacing multiple income streams. The worker who has a robust salary, in most cases will not be able to out earn that person who has numerous revenue streams thanks to having acquired passive income. Even if that healthy salary is massive in amount, there is a price to pay, albeit work. Forty hour work weeks are long enough, not to mention those who have become a slave to their day job in order to make that money that they need to keep up with the lifestyle they are chasing. Don't get me wrong, I am in no way discounting hard work. I commend you for busting your hump and getting after it. A lot can be learned and personal growth most often occurs in the trenches as we struggle. I am a firm believer that we grow through what we go through. However, I am definitely a proponent and supporter of taking time back, using it to do what one desires, and making money at the same time. How about you?

Like many things in life, as the saying goes, it is too good to be true. Y'all, when it comes to passive income, it is so good because it is so true! You better believe it if you want to live it. Now this doesn't just happen automatically overnight. Yes, it will take some capital to get started. However, you can do so little by little and over the course of time have every minute of the day be working for you. Did you know that your retirement account is a source of passive income. Every time your money compounds, you are making more and setting up your future self for success. Those index funds that Chloe invested in and her stock portfolio, you better believe it, those are some great passive income streams as well. Oh, and remember that rental property Chloe decided to purchase after marching past baby step four, another form of passive income. That $1,050 per month she was making from the duplex she owns alone is bolstering her monthly revenue stream. So let's flood our accounts and turn it up when it comes to passive income.

There are many more ways to make money in our sleep than you might think exist. Certainly, not all of these examples of passive income may apply to you and your given situation. However, like a restaurant menu, you can pick and choose the ones you wish to access. In the future, you can always add another course to this meal, the best part being that someone else will be footing the bill! I can't say this enough. I don't know about you, but I am a huge fan of food on the house so to speak. Here are some of the most common forms of passive income that wise investors are utilizing to grow their monthly cash flow…

- Dividend Stocks. ...
- Peer to Peer Lending. ...
- Rental Properties. ...
- High Yield Savings Accounts And Money Market Funds

- CD Ladders
- Annuities
- Investing spare change via Acorn or Robin Hood automatically in the Stock Market
- Invest in a REIT (Real Estate Investment Trust)
- Royalties from innovative creations (books, music, videos for example)
- App creation
- Storage Rentals
- Rent your home on Air BnB
- House Hacking (renting basement or room in your home)
- Laundromat
- CarWash
- Money Market Accounts
- Social Media Platforms
    - Youtuber
    - Instagram
    - Facebook

This list is composed of many of the viable options out there for you as a future or current passive income earner. There are others as well. Keep in mind that each of these are truly passive and require no work at all, but happen on their own. Once the capital is fronted or the idea is created, the rest is crockpot style. Set it and forget it. However, it will be hard to forget and you will greatly enjoy the checks coming in that pump your monthly income massively. Many investors and those who have reached full financial independence are at that point because passive income is what they rely on solely. Not having to work sounds like retirement. Imagine being in your forties or possibly even younger and not having to get up every day and go to the office for eight hours? That would be nice. 59.5 years old is too limiting to me and I hope that you realize that this waiting for freedom for years and years doesn't have to be this way. Just because other people in your family or neighborhood haven't tapped into passive income, that doesn't mean that you have to walk the same road of a status quo life. The easy road doesn't always lead to a dead end. Let's work smarter, not harder. With passive income streams, this is one easy road that leads to an oasis that is filled with lots of money and enables us to take our time back. We will always be able to make more money, but my philosophy has become let's make money and have all the time we desire to use doing the things we enjoy with those we love the most. Remember, it is never too late to hop on the passive income train, as this one continues to cycle through the station. Know that the wise investor, like me, will be riding it for generations to come.

CHALLENGE #8: *Acquire at least one more form of passive income*

For this challenge, I want you to access and utilize at least one additional passive income stream. You might have a number of them already or perhaps none at all. Either way, increase your monthly income by employing investment opportunities to work for you. Be the boss of your finances and allow others to do the heavy lifting, while you reap the rewards. Take a load off or for now continue to work that 9-5 but have the idea that this is not forever. Allow passive income to fuel and fund your account, grow your disposable income on a regular basis, and open up the calendar for you to do things you typically don't have time to do.

"Life isn't about waiting for the storm to pass, it's about learning to dance in the rain."

-Vivian Greene

CHAPTER 10: Insurance Safety Nets

Attack, attack, attack. These words continue to infiltrate my mind as a former collegiate athlete and basketball player. In order to win any game, you have to put points on the board. Such is life and especially when it comes to our financial situation. More money in our investment accounts and a greater net worth means we are able to get to financial freedom sooner. Being able to do what we want to do, when we want to do it, sounds awfully good to me! And yet, aggression and being on the offensive is not the only way and must not be the sole focus of building wealth and a prosperous portfolio. Inasmuch as an athlete needs to attack, playing the other side of the ball is necessary as well. Dunking the basketball might be the most glamorous thing to do on the court, slugging a grand slam on the diamond, netting a goal on the rink, and celebrating in the end zone after the game winning catch. However, as defense is a pivotal part to any game, the same holds true when it comes to our finances. So let's spend some time to dig our heels into the unglamorous, yet ever important area of insurance.

Now this is most likely the most non shiny portion of the financial world. You might be tempted to skip right over this section of the book altogether. However, I urge you to stay on the path and recall that defense will have to be played along our financial journey. Sure, it would be great that everything were smooth sailing every step of the way, but this will most likely not be the case. What insurance is all about is mitigating risk. Having a backup plan, an escape route, or a way to protect your investments and life is essential. The approach I take with insurance is that I want to have the best things in place like a bullet-proof vest to protect and shield my vitals, and yet I hope that I never have to call on it to save me. In the financial world it is like the fire in the theater example. When you go to the movies or any public venue, it is critical to know where the emergency exit is. 99.9% of the time you never will even have to think about using it to escape safely. Knowing that the safety net or backstop is there will give you more peace of mind and also assure that if that 0.1% indeed does happen, you are ready. The worst case scenario would be to have to face a tragedy during our lifetime, if there are ways to shield us from these financially, it is our responsibility to utilize them.

Neglecting insurance is a no no. Not to mention, it is against the law in many cases. Now this doesn't mean that you have to insure everything. Each purchase you make and all the electronics you buy do not require insurance, nor should you waste money on them. What I want to outline are the big areas that are going to help secure your investments, life situation, and allow you to live without that monkey on your back. No one wants to be anxious and insurance can help alleviate that in a good way. Eventually, the hope is that we get to the point where we build up enough of a net worth where we basically are able to insure ourselves. However, liability is still high especially in the day and age in which we live where lawsuits are running rampant as people are ruthless. We cannot allow someone to suck our accounts dry and not be protected.

The Big Four & More in Insurance

There are the big four when it comes to insurance and then other important areas to safeguard. It is important to grasp and not lose sight of the fact that insurance is all about transferring risk. You know the old adage, defense wins championships! When I think about some of the greatest teams of all time from my generation, they include the likes of the Chicago Bears of the 1980s in football, the New York Yankees of the 90s in baseball, Jordan's Bulls of the 90s, and the Detroit Red Wings. All of these teams won multiple titles because they locked it down on defense. In order to reach championship caliber and achieve the highest level with your finances, you must play some shut down defense. The average fan and likewise the average investor does not like this aspect at all. I am willing to bet you are thinking what I used to think, people are not flocking to stadiums to see defense played. We all enjoy the high flying offense and putting big points on the board, regardless of the sport. But like an effective General Manager of a dynasty sports team, it is super crucial to play both sides of the ball. The defense wins the title and sets the best teams apart.

Insurance is where defense lives and where you and I must invest some resources and money into. The big four when it comes to insurance are an absolute must. These insurable areas include health insurance, car insurance, life insurance, and property/homeowners. Additionally, there are other insurances that I would recommend as do the experts, such as short term & long term disability insurance, travel insurance, and identity insurance. In this chapter our goal is to provide information that will help you make better decisions, discuss the options and plans, as well as reinforce the importance as to why this less than attractive financial realm is still worthwhile.

Health Insurance

If you reside in the United States, by law you are required to have health insurance. This type of insurance is most definitely the one you will draw upon the most, especially if you have children or battle with health conditions. There are a myriad of policies, programs, and companies one can go with. If you are someone who is fortunate to hold a job with an employer who offers health insurance as part of the benefits package, consider yourself blessed. We will get into that in a little bit. According to reports from *CNBC* in the fall of 2019, a family of four was paying over $15,000 on average per year or $1,250 per month and upwards of $28,000 annually or $2,333 monthly to cover their health care. Individuals on average in 2020 have been paying $511 per month for health insurance which equates to over $6,100. Besides for this being quite expensive in terms of premiums, the specific policy really defines how much copays and deductibles will be.

The general rule of thumb when it comes to insurances, health insurance included, is that the higher the premium the lower the deductible. And of course when the premium is lower, the deductible rises. Keep in mind, the premium is the total amount or set cost that is paid out by the policyholder each month, meanwhile the deductible is a specified amount of money that the insured must pay before an insurance company will pay out a claim. We are not going to run through all the scenarios, but the bottom line is that with health insurance we need be aware of some important keys including and not limited to:

- Premiums
- Deductibles
- Out-of-pocket expenses
- Prescription drug coverage
- Health savings account eligibility
- Networks
- Available perks and benefits
- Open Enrollment Status

The more you will have to pay out of pocket on top of the premium cost must be considered. All of the above listed subsections can totally break the bank if you are not careful. However, the combined cost cannot come close to one hospital stay. Although there is nothing we should ever choose above health, people can be forced into horrible situations and become bankrupt quickly with inadequate health insurance. Cover your bases with this one. If you do not know the details of your plan that your employer offers, sit down with your HR representative and become educated. There are plenty of times when the insurance company sent me the bill when I was covered and I had to go to bat and become reimbursed. Remember, not all the crooks have guns. I am not saying that this is always intentionally done and that all insurance companies are thieves, but you have to be informed so you do not get ripped off.   As it is, we all pay more than enough for the health insurance premium we have, let's make sure it works for us when we need it to.

The best health insurance plans in my opinion are those that cover the basics in all areas including doctors visits, dental, and vision. Preventative care is typically far less expensive than when one has to be seen for something that pops up or is deemed an emergency. Most adequate health insurance plans as part of an employer benefit package are worth up to $20,000 or so per year. As a teacher for nearly a decade I was on an individual plan and then a family plan where I paid in a range of $150-$300 per month. This is extremely cheap thanks to the benefit package and the insurance was really good being what is called a 90/10 plan, meaning that I was covered for the first 90% of claims with a $0 deductible and then had to pick up the next 10% up to a certain dollar amount. The insurance company then covered the rest fully, no matter what the total amount was. Out of pocket in a ten year period, I paid a few hundred dollars max and that was for medical, dental, and vision combined. Granted we were in good health and young, but what I want to stress is the importance of job security that includes benefits such as health insurance.

HSA

The final thing to note in this territory, which we are covering on a macro level and with brevity, is that you can utilize an HSA. An HSA is a Health Savings Account. An HSA is a tax-advantaged medical savings account available to taxpayers in the U.S. who are enrolled in a high-deductible health plan. The funds contributed to this type of account are not subject to federal income tax at the time of deposit, which is a huge advantage. It is tax free money. The limits in 2020 for an individual and family for an HSA are $3,550 and $7,100 respectively.

For patrons above 55 years of age there is a catch up program limit of $1,000 in additional funds. Not all health insurance plans are eligible for the HSA and in order to know if yours is it must have a high deductible and meet the following requirements according to IRS regulations: 1) a deductible of at least $1,400 for self-only coverage or $2,800 for family coverage and 2) an out-of-pocket maximum that is below a $6,900 threshold for single-only coverage or $13,800 limit for family coverage. The money in an HSA is then used to offset medical costs for any bills that might come up and many people as they increase in age or grow a family tend to use these funds. HSA fund dollars are most often used to pay deductibles and non covered expenses for vision and dental work. If you wish to withdraw money out of this account, you are required to pay taxes at your income tax rate on top of a 10% penalty.

Life Insurance

How much money would you put on the value of your life? Life itself is definitely priceless, however when it comes to life insurance whatever you sign up for will be paid out when you die. Well, not everything. Along with writing a last will testament, there are certain things that you must do especially once you get married or have children. This includes buying into a life insurance policy. This might be the most lucrative area of them all outside of health insurance for the companies who want to dig into your pockets. There are two main types of life insurance policies, namely term-life and whole life. One is very good and extremely beneficial, costs are fairly low, and coverage is high. Sounds like a good deal right? That is because it is. The major difference between the two is that term life insurance policies have no cash value until you or your spouse passes away, while a whole life policy accumulates value over time while you are alive and payout according to the premiums you paid at the point of death. This makes your whole life policy option seem attractive and if you get hooked by an insurance broker, they will definitely try to reel you in for their big catch. Their big catch, meaning what I would like to stress. We will break it down below with specificity. In short, term life insurance is the way to go and the only one that I would endorse or recommend to people out there because your money has much greater earning potential in other vehicles. Remember, insurance is not an investment or offensive approach, it is playing defense. However, I must pass on the knowledge of both insurances, including whole life policies so that you understand in the ins and outs. Like with everything, the choice is ultimately yours, but I believe that soon you will understand why I prefer the term policy as opposed to whole life.

Term Life Insurance

I took out my first term life policy shortly after I got married at the age of 25. It was a great choice on my part. My wife also got a term life policy. No, we both certainly do not plan to kick the can anytime soon, but if death were to come to one of us we would be covered. A term life policy by definition is a life insurance plan that is good for a set length of time or term. You can buy a ten year term life plan, a twenty year one, and so on. For those of you out there who are younger in age and in good health like we were, these plans are as cheap as $140 per year, sometimes less and provide upwards of $500,000 of coverage. Enter Chloe, stage right. Remember her? Well, she is now getting married and ready to purchase a life insurance policy. Chloe contacts a number of companies and settles on AIG Direct, a very reputable company. Since she is in good health and fairly young, she and her fiance get policies set up so they can go into place as soon as they are married. Chloe's comes in at less than $14 a month. She signs a ten year term and it gets her half a million dollars in coverage. Her future husband will get the same. Over the decade of the policy, Chloe will have paid out less than $1,700 total, $170 or so per year. If she were to pass away or her husband were to die, the widowed spouse would get a complete and total payout of $500,000 upon death. This is a very inexpensive way to cover your significant other or the other big stake holder in your household if tragedy were to occur. You can apply for and sign up with a longer term, but when you re-up if you do it will cost you more. As one's age climbs, the next term is higher because the chances of death also increase. For those of you with families with children, it is wise to get a policy that is worth more perhaps $1,000,000. A good guideline to follow in terms of coverage is to get a policy that is worth 10-15 times your income level. Remember, it is life insurance not investment insurance and is something that hopefully we never have to use, but if doomsday came knocking our family would have all bases covered.

Whole Life Insurance

Whole life insurance involves what the name suggests, your whole life. So why wouldn't you want your whole life covered? After all, you are precious beyond your last breath. This is completely true and I totally agree, except for the part where you are covered for your whole life and how much you will end up paying into the plan. Whole life insurance policies depending on your age and gender range can cost five to fifteen times more monthly and annually than term life coverage. Therefore, taking *MetLife* policies with $250,000 worth of coverage, the cost per month for a healthy male comes in at nearly $2,000 and for females around $1,800. For a year that would mean paying out nearly $24,000. For people who reach 40 years of age you can tack on another $1,000 monthly for sure. That is crazy!! We are talking about life insurance. Whole life policies have what is called cash value components. What this means is that the extra money that you paid into the policy is available down the line and grows incrementally as time goes on. The graphic below gives a nice visual of how this whole life cash value works. In essence, the policy premium is 10-15 times more expensive per month because this money is being used as an investment for you to be able to access down the road. For those of you who might be wondering why is money set aside to be used later on bad, keep in mind that you are able to gain a whole lot more in interest earnings with the other vehicles out there. Enter Chloe, stage left. She was presented the option of this whole life policy when she spoke with the insurance agent at AIG because this is their big win on commission. An agent doesn't make much on a policy, term policy that is, which only brings in $14 per month or less than $170 for an entire year. They do however, with one that is raking in 15Xs that per month. Why the company always wants the customer to go with a whole life policy is pretty easy to see. The other nugget of information that is not revealed, unless you specifically ask for it, and even then it will be glossed over, is that the amount of interest returned to you on your investment on the whole life policy is actually pitiful. Most whole life policies net a dividend interest yield of 1.5%-3.2% annually. That comes in at an average of 2.35% per year. In most cases it doesn't even cover inflation!! You might be thinking, wow this is a very one sided argument. I believe that is because it is. Why would you not take the $1,700-$2,000 a month extra, put it into a great index fund or spread it out amongst great ETFs or stocks and bonds and have it grow three 3-4 times the amount in interest? All of these thoughts were running rampant in Chloe's mind, as she has become a wise investor over the years. As Chloe exits the room, stage right, she is very happy with the decision to go with the ten year term policy.   You can clearly see at this juncture it is a no brainer. My hope is that you will STAY AWAY from whole life policies. Dave Ramsey calls them dumb, stupid, and insane! He is right. No one is getting rich off of whole life insurance policy. The agent tosses the bait out there, tries to paint a great picture, begins to reel you in and before you know it, you are being convinced that something you will pay into for decades is a good idea! There is a reason why they call it a whole life policy and it is not because it covers you for your whole life. My take is that it is because you pay in and are taken advantage of for your whole lifetime. Oh and don't let anyone talk you into that this is a great tax benefit option, there are so many others out there far better. Salesmen want to make sales, they are not looking out for your investment, unless they profit which is a win for them.

At the end of the day, life insurance has one job and that is to cover the loss of life in the midst of death. This is not an investment tool or option nor should it be spun that way. Cover your bases and have a backstop in place to be fully prepared. I will continue to have a term life policy and as my family grows I will increase the bottom line coverage amount. The term policy premium will increase as my age rises, but that is quite alright, as it will always be a mere fraction of the cost of whole life and the interest, as well as cash flow coming from real estate and other investments will cover this easily along the way.

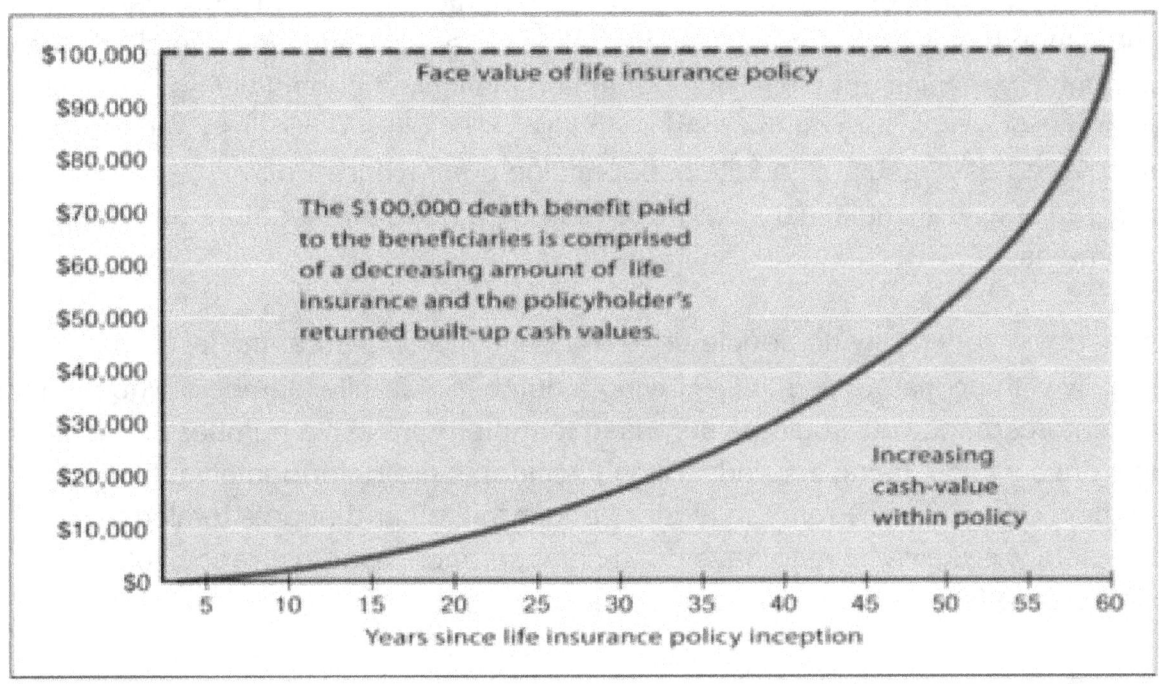

Car Insurance

Pulling out of the driveway in her Toyota Corolla, Chloe was on her way to work for another big day at XCompany where she had a few presentations to make to potential clients. As she listened to some soft tunes on her radio and went through her main talking points, she was ready to knock it out of the park. Landing a couple more large accounts would allow her to hit the numbers she was projecting for the month. While more than halfway to her work site, she pumped the brakes and came to a crawling halt at the red light in front of her. She was sitting there peacefully when she looked into her rearview mirror and a mid size SUV came barreling into her at 40mph. Thankfully, Chloe was uninjured in the accident and to no fault of her own, her car was smashed up and not driveable. As it was being towed away she was a little bit saddened, but didn't sweat it since she had great car insurance and was covered. The inexperienced teen who had hit her however, was driving an underinsured vehicle and that would be problematic for that party, who was having anything but a fiesta on that day.

Car insurance is something that we all need and it is the one area that will most likely be drawn upon than any other insurance we have, besides for health care. There is a far greater probability that we will get into an accident while behind the wheel than in any other form of transportation. We drive and we drive often. The amount of variables out there, not to mention the lack of control we have with the other millions of drivers on the road is endless. People are reckless and we must be covered as a result. In addition, depending upon where we live geographically, animals, especially deer can be a huge infringement on our daily commutes.

Nowadays, very rarely do people drive without collision insurance, let alone illegally with no insurance at all. Having a number of family members who are in law enforcement, you would be surprised that there are still a number of people who drive without being insured. Yikes! Accidents are unfortunately a fairly frequent occurrence. From the fender bender to the car that gets totaled in a complete wreck, we have to have good car insurance. Car insurance 101 really involves the following six coverages:

- Bodily Injury Liability
- Medical Payments or Personal Injury Protection (PIP)
- Property Damage Liability
- Collision
- Comprehensive
- Uninsured and Underinsured Motorist Coverage

Certainly, by shopping around and combining your homeowners/property insurance along with your car insurance policy, this can help save some bucks. However, a lot of the cost has to do with one's driving record, as well as gender and age. Sorry guys, for some reason they think we are a bit more reckless behind the wheel. I can't imagine why. So it literally pays to drive well and drive safely. Breaking down the top six portions of an auto policy further, we will find that there are some a car owner will want to pay even closer attention to than others. I am willing to bet that the majority of people out there and that includes those reading this book, probably do not know what exactly is included in their policy. Now I am not suggesting you go home and memorize your entire car insurance plan, but it is a good idea to know what is covered and how much is covered so that you can decide whether you are adequately protected or not.

Bodily injury liability involves the persons who become hurt in the crash and how much coverage there is to cover any lawsuit that could occur as a result of those injuries. I would suggest having upwards of $300,000 as we all know how expensive medical procedures and bills can be. The second is a similar category (PIP), covering medical payments, meaning a couple hundred thousand minimum should be in place. Property damage liability should be set around $100,000 to cover any damages. For collision I would suggest a $500 deductible. This will keep your total premium at a moderate rate, but also give you the affordability factor on the other end if your car gets banged up. In a similar plan you would be on the hook to pay the first $500 and then the rest is covered by your insurance company. Comprehensive insurance allows you as the vehicle owner to have your car repaired if damaged outside of a collision. Full coverage for this is important to have. Lastly, having uninsured and underinsured motorist coverage is vital. For Chloe this was the one that really saved the day, as the damage to her car committed by the uninsured teen did not cost her extra or a massive unending headache.

For those of you out there who are still having a tough time letting go of that high end vehicle, keep in mind this is another factor that keeps your insurance rates higher. I am not saying to drive around an old beater, but the higher the value of the vehicle, the more your premium will be. Leasing vehicles lends to higher premium rates as well. In addition, you will most likely be a whole lot more upset if your 2020 Mercedes Benz GLE 450, with a sticker price base of $85,000, gets a scratch, let alone in a major accident. Driving a more modest vehicle helps out in so many ways including when paying the insurance bill.

Short Term & Long Term Disability Insurance

As I grow in wisdom and learn more about my own finances including the sectors of this all important realm, disability insurance becomes an important one to possess. Considering there are many careers where one has a greater likelihood of severe injury or a job ending due to the nature of the work that is done, this one can be purchased at a reasonable cost. For those of you who are in any kind of emergency response field, including police, fire, EMT, search and rescue, military, or are in a construction oriented field, this is a very good policy to hold. Frankly, I recommend it to anyone, especially those who have children as expenses would be nearly impossible without that income stream. Long-term disability insurance covers a portion of one's income, usually between 50-70%. This coverage goes into effect when someone has become injured or seriously ill and can no longer work for an extended period of time. The long-term disability plan will help to cover a part of the salary of the employee. Short-term disability is very similar, just the time table for how long one is out of work is far less. For a long-term policy, the benefits can last until the worker can go back to work or for the duration of time that is outlined and stated in the policy. Some policies pay out for X amount of years or at times as long as you are disabled until age 65. Of course the premium is higher for these policies. For short term policies, they typically pay out for 3-6 months or up to a year max. The average cost of such disability policies which are most often coupled together are 1-3% of your annual gross income level. Chloe who is now making $75,000 for XCompany would be paying out somewhere in the ballpark range of $750-$2,000 or so per year. When broken down that can be as little as $33 per paycheck. Well worth getting for the worker who is more "at risk" due to higher danger on the job, as well as anyone for that matter to cover your back.

Homeowners Insurance

Owning a home is a great investment as we discussed earlier. As is holding stake in a rental property. Along with owning a home comes yearly expenses such as property insurance to protect your assets. Homeowners policies typically cover damage and destruction to one's residence including the exterior and interior. These policies also include covering any losses that are a result of damaged or stolen possessions, as well as personal liability for harm to people who visit one's home. Three basic levels of coverage exist in most policies: 1) actual cash value, 2) replacement cost, and 3) extended replacement cost or value. Like the others we have discussed in this chapter, the higher the total value one is insuring, the higher the premium will be. Geographical location also comes into play, as some areas are much more susceptible to various kinds of weather, damage, or other factors like crime. The area that should be focused most on is holding at least $300,000-$500,000 in liability insurance to cover any potential lawsuits. I would get a policy with a higher deductible rate since damage to the home if a tree falls on it or some other large issue will most likely be quite expensive anyway. It is not likely, unless you live in a disaster zone, along the coast, an earthquake region or wildfire area. In that case, it is really important to know whether or not your homeowners policy covers these natural disasters. If it does, super. If not I would get the extra coverage based on where you live and the probability of something happening. A house fire can happen, however it is more likely to have water damage due to flooding or hurricanes in Florida along a beachfront property for example. Replacement cost involves how much the house you live in or property would be to build again from start to finish. Having more than the value of the home is a good rule of thumb, especially if the home was built decades ago. For example, Chloe has an additional $40,000 of coverage (on top of the current value assessment of her house) on replacement cost as her home was built in the 1970s. Homes back then and even the appraised amount today is not going to be how much the actual cost is to replace the residence. For the investors out there who are still renting, pick up a quick renter's insurance policy to cover any damages to your apartment or stolen/damaged property. If you are the landlord, like Chloe is, insure your property as if it were the one you were living in full time. After all, at the end of the day it is your property and this investment should be safeguard in the same way. Of course, personal property can be insured in the same type of way as one's home or the belongings are covered. If you have other property or personal items that are of great value in a different location outside of your home, you may wish to purchase additional property insurance for those items.

Travel Insurance

The alarm clock is set for 5am and it is the night before Chloe is to leave for her anniversary trip with her husband to Europe. They have been saving up and planning for this vacation for a while. The day is almost here and she is so excited. Dinner by the Eiffel Tower, four nights on the Amalfi Coast, riding in a gondola in Venice and laying out on the beautiful beaches of Santorini, Greece. This is just one more benefit of having a firm grip on one's finances in order to be able to indulge in such a luxurious vacation! In a number of hours it will be time to go to the airport for that trip of a lifetime. Chloe's bags are packed and her husband is just as enthused as she is to go away. When the couple wakes up the next morning it quickly turns from excitement to nightmare. It is an awful lot brighter than the norm for 5am. Then in a split second, Chloe glances over at her battery operated alarm clock and notices that is blank. She scrambles to her phone, which reads 7:32 am. There was no way they would make it for their 8am flight! What happened? This and many other reasons are why purchasing travelers insurance when taking a big trip is appropriate. You will find a number of people who argue against it, but having peace of mind for an additional $100-$200 when you are laying out nearly $10K is pretty wise if you ask me. Since Chloe has gained wisdom, although disappointed that they missed their flight, their situation is no problem. She and her husband can hop on the next flight at Noon and be at their destination a few hours later than originally expected. Without insurance, she would have lost out on thousands in airfare and really had been kicking herself. Travelers insurance is a great way to protect your trip beforehand, while on vacation, and on the route home. I recall a time my family went to Europe and were set to disembark on a 12 day European cruise. The flights were delayed due to inclement weather from one of our departing cities and we missed the boat. Literally, our cruise ship took off without us. Talk about sinking one's vacation plans! Oh and did I mention, our bags got lost as well. So when we finally arrived at the second port of call a number of days later by flying to the next cruise stop to catch our ship, we had no luggage. Fortunately, trip insurance covered us buying a wardrobe, reimbursed us for the missed time on the boat, and took care of all the expenses to get to the next country. Without it, we would have been losing out on thousands of dollars. For smaller trips, I don't recommend travel insurance as much, but it can't hurt and is really up to you. Something to consider is if you have enough money to go away, a few extra dollars won't break the bank to have that trip insured. It's amazing that the rain always seems to fall on and find the person without an umbrella. Do yourself a favor and stay dry, be insured.

Identity Theft Insurance

The 21st Century is an era that is completely tech driven. There are countless benefits to this, yet one big detriment named identity theft. People are no longer just stealing our stuff, but they are so cut throat they go after our identity. This can be extremely taxing to an individual who is not covered, let alone very costly. The headache that goes into recovering one's identity after it is compromised is massive. The cost is typically between $25-$50 per year for identity theft insurance and most policies cover upwards of $25,000 to cover legal fees and agencies that work toward cleaning things up and getting your identity back. Right about now, I'm thinking who the heck would want to be me? Really, I'm just saying. Well, I will only speak for myself on that one. Haha. Unfortunately, scammers are going to keep working the system and try to pawn money and people's identities because they don't want to work hard for a living. Do yourself another favor and protect yourself. Cyber crime is the new age wild west cowboy.

Now that we have covered the basics of defensive tactics, namely insurances, it is clear to see why this is so crucial for us and how safeguarding our finances brings peace to our lives. Insurance, namely playing defense, is not fun in most cases, but necessary. A winning portfolio has a protective shell around it. As you continue to accumulate wealth and build your net worth, it will eventually be smart to acquire a personal insurance umbrella policy. This is to protect you against people who are on the hunt to expose you and make a lot of money because they somehow gain wind of your financial situation. Nobody wants to have a target on their back, but it is especially uninviting and unwelcome when we have more to lose. Insure yourself and your assets because the one time we don't, it seems that the "bad luck" has a way of finding us. Tilt the scales in your favor by playing strong defense and you can live worry free.

CHALLENGE #9: *Do a total assessment of your insurance policies & get coverage.*

This challenge is not going to be fun in the least, but it is important. Take some time over the next week and do a total assessment of all of the insurance policies you hold. Use this chapter's subtitles and the checklist below to ensure that you are insured in all the right areas. If you have these backstops in place, certify that they are covering yourself adequately enough based on the recommended numbers in this chapter. If for some reason one or more of these areas of insurance have not been purchased, build this into your budget making the necessary adjustments.

Insurance Checklist:

1) **Health Insurance**
    -**Medical**
    -**Dental**
    -**Vision**

2) **Life Insurance**

3) Homeowners Insurance

4) Car Insurance

5) Disability Insurance

6) Identity Theft Insurance

7) Travelers Insurance (optional, but highly recommended when traveling)

"Too many people spend money they haven't earned, to buy things they don't want, to impress people they don't like."

-Will Smith

CHAPTER 11: Data Dive

Part of this journey and compiling the best financial resources for people out there, was to ask a variety of Americans what they felt were the top areas to unshell in the world of finance. In this chapter we will uncover how many people feel and what they wished they knew about earlier to avoid set back with regard to their money. What my qualitative and quantitative research found after in depth analysis, interviews, and compiling data across the lower to higher middle class sector of society was pretty amazing. I had a few hypotheses that turned out to be spot on and yet the collective and individual responses of people I encountered were quite alarming. All in all, the data and statistics revealed that five essential things stood out most to hard working citizens when it comes to what they wished they knew earlier or had more knowledge on and they are as follows:

1) The importance of beginning early with investments to maximize compound interest.
2) The significance of saving for retirement from the beginning of one's working career.
3) Living on a budget and understanding the importance of a written game plan.
4) Avoiding debt at all costs.
5) Understanding student loans before signing and navigating credit.

If people would only heed the advice that this data dive has inspired, the majority of Americans would not be in debt and would be much more financially free. These five major categories were the culmination of responses by people across various races, religions, genders, and age ranges. What the data told me was that most people out there, when they are honest about money, have made mistakes and do want to be successful. However, the question that remains is, how badly do they really want it? Like anything, it is easier to talk about it than be about it. The end result of having $1.5-$2 million dollars stacked up in one's retirement or investment accounts at the end of 30-35 years of working sounds phenomenal. Let me get on that plan most people would say. And yet, they are not willing to chip away, month by month, year after year, in order to accumulate that growth. Not having bank accounts bleeding with debt sounds terrific. People claim they want a better life, yet the lack of discipline and focus derails them and they end up under a mountain of debt. Ambition and dreams, goals and desires for a great career by going away to college sounds fantastic. Student loan debt soon becomes a mortgage payment after flipping the tassel and walking the stage as the college graduate is anywhere but close to acquiring a home of their own. Around and around on the hamster wheel we go, a vicious cycle. Why? Why do we continue to not pay heed to the advice of those who know better and have developed a plan that works. Why not at least implement even some of this knowledge? That continues to boggle my mind. Let's take a closer look into these five specific areas that the data has shown are the most critical according to mainstream Americans with regard to understanding finances and winning with money. It's time to jump into the data jacuzzi!

1.Begin Early & Let Compound Interest do its Magic

After computing all of the data findings that my team and I collected, reading survey results, and interviewing many hard working Americans, I was pleasantly surprised to learn that the number one aspect or trend was the need for one to get into the game early with investments. We spent ample time on compound interest in the previous chapters. However, this is something that I want to dig even deeper into, here with you, and share some thoughts by your peers out there. When I teach my financial course and show people how to utilize various winning financial strategies. There comes a time in the class I teach that I use the Financial Peace University example of Jack and Blake, which is pictured below. These two brothers, how much they each decide to invest, and most importantly when they begin investing paints a crystal clear picture that proves why getting started early is key! Jack is a wise investor, he learned from an early age and heeded the advice of this book, as well as sound experts in the field. At 21, Jack began investing $2,400 every year, simply putting away $200 a month. Nothing crazy, but a great disciplined approach from a young age. By the time he turned 30 years old, Jack was married, bought a house, and had a baby on the way. He stopped investing due to these large life changes. In essence, Jack stopped contributing to his investment, however, his money did not stop!! Blake on the other hand, decided to live beyond his means, using up all the disposable cash he had and did not invest a dime until he turned 30. As Blake matured, he realized that driving those fancy cars and going out to eat all the time was not going to make him wealthy. Although he did not acquire debt per say, he had nothing to show for his first 9 years of working. From age 30 to age 67, that is almost 40 years, Blake decided to put away $2,400 every year or $200 per month. He grew in discipline and thought that he would be fine in the long run. Blake ended up making a total investment of $91,200 which grew to a whopping $1,483,033! Well done. On the other hand, Jack who only put in $21,600 which is almost 5X less than his brother Blake, has a total nest egg of $2,547,150!! WHAT!!! That is insane! You are telling me that by starting 9 years earlier, making a small contribution of $200 per month for less than 10 years ballooned to 1.5X the amount of money even though Blake invested 28 years less than his brother? You better believe it! This is a prime example of why getting in the game and allowing your greatest advocate, father time, to work for you when it comes to compound interest. If you have not started, today is the day to begin! For those of you who are parents out there teach your kids. For the others who have younger siblings, nieces or nephews, please inform them!

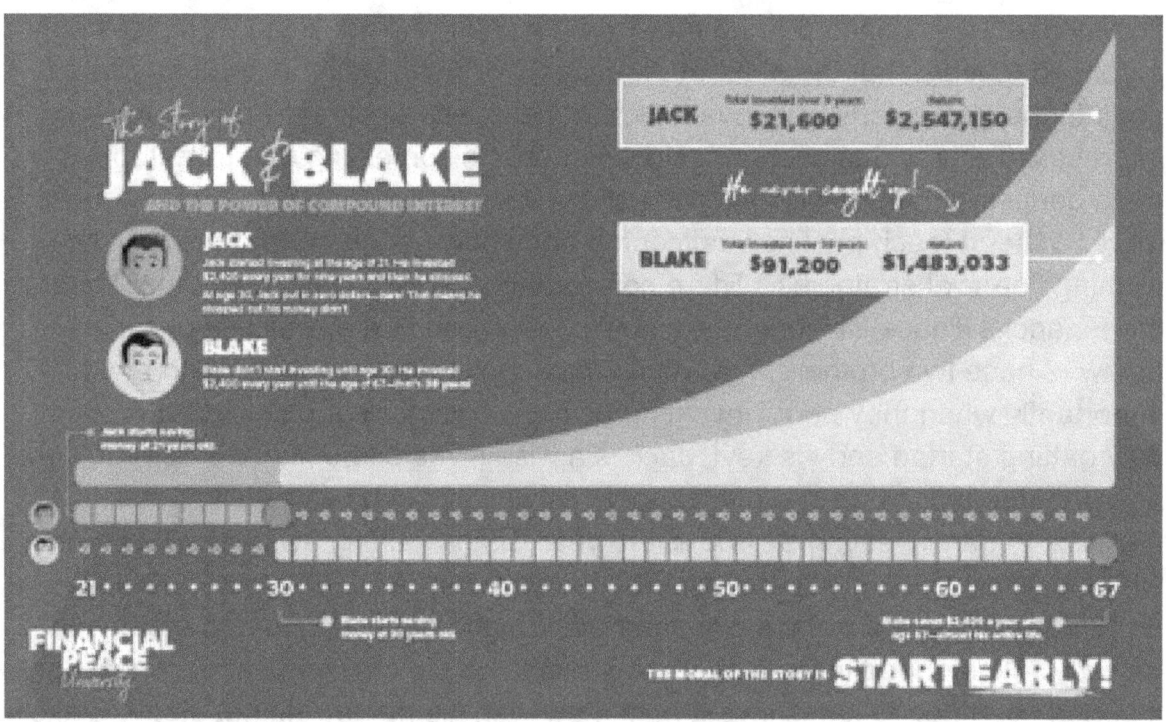

A number of years ago my wife's cousins turned 18 and 19 respectfully. I picked them up along with their boyfriends and brought them with me to set up a Roth IRA. The girls have been contributing ever since. I explained to them about how important it was to begin early, even by putting in just a little bit each month. It is incredible how their portfolios have grown over the past few years. This set of sisters is learning that compound interest will do crazy things because they started so young! Here is what some of the people I surveyed had to say about getting started early:

"Start early, compound interest works well." -Rick, business owner for 30 years and former pro baseball player, age 56.

"I wish I started when I was 22 instead of 42. The new house, kids, and bills got in the way and sometimes you don't have anything left." -Bill from New York, age 52

2. Saving for Retirement

Going hand in hand with getting in the game early and utilizing compound interest, is saving for retirement. Getting started early and often is the name of this game. I would like to believe that most people have good intentions in mind to start a retirement fund down the road. This is a very popular response. Many of you out there might think similarly and fall back on the fact that you are young and have plenty of time. However, before people know it, they are in their 40s or even 50 years of age without a dollar in their retirement account. You might as well walk the plank at that point! Maybe that is a bit harsh because as I mentioned in previous chapters that there are ways to try to catch back up. However, the point that needs to be made is that retirement planning and saving must be taken much more seriously. The conclusion I reach for the reason why so many people wish they started right off the rip or much earlier is because as the years go by and expenses pile up, it becomes more difficult to establish this habit. For those who sock away money each month from the beginning, it becomes routine and is easy to continue to do so as it is a choice that is nearly put on autopilot. You saw the magnitude of compound interest in the last example mentioned in the previous section. Whether you build your 401K, take advantage of your employer's match, start investing in a Roth IRA or some other long term retirement fund, you are building a winning future. Most Americans don't think about it until it is far too late, let alone do they start contributing. A recent survey has found that 42% of Americans have saved $10,000 or less for retirement, while 14% have absolutely no money put away. The numbers continue to show that over 64% of Americans are not ready for retirement due to a lack of funds being saved. My hope is that you will fall into the top percentage of people who are not only prepared, but can retire earlier than the norm because you got in on the game early, putting money away in a responsible manner. Remember, the goal is to contribute at least 15% of your annual income once you complete baby step two of becoming debt free besides the mortgage and have a fully emergency fund established. My hope is that for many of you, your retirement switch will get flipped on even sooner. Let's take a moment to hear what a couple of people had to say when interviewed about retirement planning and getting into the game earlier.

"I wished I would have known earlier and started investing in my 403(b), Roth, & stocks in my early 20s. I wish I would have surrounded myself with people who are smarter than me, especially in finances." -Ady, Bronx, NY, age 36.

"If I knew at age 21 that I now know today at age 31, I would have stockpiled my retirement accounts and would be well over a hundred thousand dollars ahead of where I am currently at. I wish I could go back and redo this area of my life. But the fact is there are no mulligans when it comes to finances. Beginning ten years sooner would have provided my future self with well over a million dollars more than I will have when it is all said and done because of compound interest." - Jason, Entrepreneur, age 31.

3. Living on a Budget

Again, I was pleasantly surprised that the number three thing people wished they knew earlier was why and how to live on a budget. At this point you know how to formulate your monthly budget and why it is so crucial to stick to this financial blueprint. So let's take a look at what some of the people out there had to say regarding budgeting.

"The number one thing is to learn how to budget your monthly finances, including pay your bills and set money aside for entertainment or fun things." Tom, U.S. Navy Veteran, age 75.

"I hated living on a budget, but it allowed us to pay off debt and our home. We now will be able to do things that most people aren't able to do at such a young age." -Lanay, age 30.

"The envelope system works, we have been using it for over 50 years." -Vera, grandmother of 11, age 80.

"Always have an updated budget spreadsheet with all your income and your bills listed. On this sheet track every penny you make and spend, adjust accordingly."- Melissa, mother & school counselor, age 40

As you can see, people who are asked about the important things when it comes to finances mentioned budgeting. Some probably wished they developed one much earlier, while others admitted that it is a must even if it is not always fun. I believe that living on a budget helps you to stay on course and is essential no matter what income bracket you fall within. It is the number one thing people need to do to have success with their money. Let me state that again, developing and using a budget is the most important aspect of developing winning habits and winning with your money! It doesn't matter how much you make, but is way more about what you do with what you make. Being a good steward with our income will allow us to maximize all of the many opportunities that are out there including investments and retirement. Ultimately what we do each day will have a profound impact and write the chapter of our lives years to come. If people desire to reach financial freedom and true peace with money, they must budget. Without a written game plan, it is nearly impossible to win with money.

4. Avoiding Debt

"I wish I knew what the real value of money is. I wish I was exposed to how important money is in our daily lives." Hunter, college student, age 19

"but whatever I made, I saved up or spent on gas, movies, fun with friends. It just simply didn't occur to me, how or what I spent money on. Honestly I had no real understanding of credit or financial literacy." -Kathryn, Long Island, NY, age 33

Not knowing what the cost of debt is can be a gigantic problem. Debt is dumb and is something that must not become our friend. When I was listening to the Dave Ramsey show on the radio during my drive to work, it was funny that he said that debt has become like people's pets. It is always lingering around, sticking by our side, and you can't get rid of it. This doesn't have to be the case, nor should it be our norm. There is a reason why the fourth suggestion based on the research study was to avoid debt. I believe that it would have come in higher on the scale if people weren't so programmed to think that it is "simply a part of life." Just because something has become normalized doesn't mean it is good or should be the way we choose to live. After all, I remind you, normalcy hasn't gotten the average American far in the world of finances, well besides leaving them behind the eight ball and in debt that is. Doing things radically different, choosing to live in an uncommon manner like nobody else does or wants to is what I am talking about. Now, that sacrifice is what gets some serious results. In the coming chapters we will discuss debt in more detail, especially when it comes to navigating the college scene and the student loan crisis in America.   For now however, it is important to point out that young people and old people alike have encountered debt and this four letter word is something that can completely drain us.

Most people probably don't think about how compound interest works in the opposite direction when it comes to debt. That amazing eighth wonder of the world quickly becomes your greatest nightmare when you are piling up the debt. So why don't we have more knowledge on these topics, especially important one's this chapter has exposed, in this case debt? Negative roadblocks like debt can create a huge chasm between where we are at today and our future aspirations of achieving financial freedom. Debt creates a massive impingement on us and makes it tougher to meander the everyday life we live. Let's face it and call a spade a spade, debt is the key factor that often tends to be our greatest area of struggle or causes the largest setback. Is it because people really don't know better? In some cases and to a point this is probably true. However, much of it comes down to my favorite word in this financial program. That word is DISCIPLINE. Staying disciplined is what allows you to win and lacking it leads to stupid spending decisions, derailment from your budget and all of this will tend to land someone facedown in the debt snow bank. Focus is hard to do 24/7 and 365 days a year. It is my understanding that this data and the people I have spoken with show us, yet again, that living with discipline is much more feasible when we have a budget. However, we must tackle debt and understand the enemy well. Debt seems to come crashing in on our lives far too often. Most of the time we are the ones who invite it to the party. It is time to hold onto what we make and be smart with our money. Don't fall off course or take the reins away by not having a plan. Otherwise, the ugly red monster will consume your finances and all the green you have labored so hard for.

5. Understanding Student Loans & Credit

The fifth topic that continued to appear during the deep data drive was the topic of student loans and credit. Time to really jump into the jacuzzi. Come on y'all, what are you waiting for? You know how it is, everyone is drinking that Kool Aid and hopping into the college realm just like a late night summer BBQ where we plunge into the whirlpool without thinking twice. Let's start with the latter, namely credit and then work our way into the educational hot tub known as college. Credit is something that we do need if we desire to borrow money. The ideal situation is to not have to borrow much at all and to pay outright by utilizing cash flow principles. For the sake of argument, I will say that at every stage of the game this is not completely realistic. When purchasing a house for example, most people would have to save for over 20 years to be able to buy their home with cash. Meanwhile, renting is building no equity either. A lose lose you say? Well let's take a closer look and find the balance by unveiling the tale of the tape. Credit is something that we all do need. Whether it is a big purchase like a house or buying a car, building responsible credit is beneficial if done in the right manner. Having no credit at all can leave someone in a bad spot or tough situation. Not to mention, drowning in debt and falling behind will certainly hurt your credit score for years to come, as credit involves the trust factor between the lender and the borrower.

Courtney from Maryland had this to say regarding credit, "My parents and nobody ever talked to me about when and how to build credit history. Then when I graduated college all of a sudden people were looking at my credit to sign a lease and buy a car and I was in trouble...Even a lack of credit history will wind you up with a much higher loan rate on things like a car or a house and can cost you big in the long run....I wish I knew this at 16-18 years old." So why didn't Courtney know this? Whose responsibility is it to teach younger people? This book is not about the education system, but I believe that in every high school in America there should be a class that teaches students about all of these financial topics on a broad scale. This theme of ignorance and not being informed runs deep. Diana from the Dominican Republic had this to say about credit and student loans, "Well if I go back to my earlier days, school loans. I wasn't very informed while in college on taking out student loans. Also looking back at my younger years, credit."

Furthermore, student loans are certainly robbing mere kids decades of their lives. I cannot imagine leaving college today with a four year degree for something like being a teacher or another mid level entry paying job. Nowadays, having to pay off hundreds of thousands of dollars in student loan debt is absurd. It doesn't make sense. It is stupid and wrong all at the same time. Education and knowledge is an extremely valuable thing. As a former teacher for nearly a decade, again, I can attest to this the most. There is a price we can put and must place on education though and one that we should not exceed. Let alone, there is a limit that we must not allow young people to sign their life away to because that is exactly what is happening. Society has crossed the line! The majority of college students don't comprehend the amount of debt that they are accruing while earning their degree. It is probably because on top of their studies, college kids are learning about life, are deep in personal growth, and of course are having fun with their friends. It isn't until after the fact when that monthly bill comes due that it's like, "Oh shoot, now what?" Baby step five and the college situation is something we must examine because there is a far better way than what continues to go on in this country. The following chapter will take us into the world of the college situation and explore a realm that has become out of freaking control.

CHALLENGE #10: Choose at least two areas from the data dive & become an expert in them.

My next challenge for you is to take the list of these top five areas where people wished they knew more about from the start and become an expert on them. Pick two that you particularly don't know that much about. Read a number of books on those topics and then put your increased knowledge to good use. In addition, share what you learn with others, especially those you love most. Spread the knowledge and better someone else's life that you care about. Pay it forward to the next generation. This is just one way to make the world better and to improve the life of another person.

"College costs are out of control."

-President Donald Trump

CHAPTER 12:
Baby Step 5 & Student Loans

It was late August, the car was packed and I was excited to be going away for the first time. In three hours we would be at Le Moyne College in Syracuse, NY where I would call home for the next five and a half years. At 17 years of age there was only one thing on my mind, making friends. Sure, I was excited to begin learning at the collegiate level, but I hoped that I could find a crew to hang with quickly. There is a major problem that is happening in our country today, a national epidemic. I am not talking about another wave of Coronavirus. The sickness that is plaguing our society is the ill conceived notion that everyone must go to college. Many job markets are so flooded, degrees cost ungodly amounts, and teenagers have no clue what the heck they want to do with their life. This is all a recipe for financial disaster. On the other hand, it is the debt of the young college student that keeps universities and schools across America growing richer and richer. To me it is very disturbing and something must be done to cut the cost of higher education. I don't believe we should take the Bernie Sanders, free education approach. But I am not discussing politics here, it is about a financial crisis that continues to build and shows no signs of slowing down. Until the government and leaders of our country make amends and change this monstrous situation, we must educate students in high school about the evil villain named Sallie Mae and a better way to navigate the college debacle.

My youngest cousin just finished his first year of school at Wagner College in Staten Island. I am so proud of him for how hard he worked to earn numerous scholarships due to his efforts in the classroom and his great leadership skills he implemented when his nose wasn't in the books. As a result of hard work and focus, this young man will help lighten the load of his college expenses. Not to mention, he is working and paying for much of the rest of the costs he endures as he goes through school. Most people believe that it is impossible to cash flow college. However, it is not. A four year degree these days still has value, but in many cases it has become almost obsolete. The majority of people to get into higher earning careers most often need to pursue a master's degree or higher to reach that next echelon. In this chapter we are going to talk about college, how to educate our young people in terms of student loans and debt, ways to minimize costs, as well as why college is not for everyone. Oh yeah, one more thing, we will speak about baby step five.

Baby step five involves saving money for your kid's college education. Now this is a matter of preference and choice. Some of you might be thinking, *If my kid wants to go away to school that is a choice I will support, but the degree, I just can't afford.* As the minister in the Church so emphatically says, "Can I get an Amen?" All jokes aside however, college costs are just much too high for countless parents. Let's face it, they themselves are paying off their own loans, mortgages, and monthly bills before they even consider another never ending college payment carousel ride from their kids. It is certainly not a must, to pay for your child's education and in many situations it might not even be an option at all. Nonetheless, I do want to talk about it because some of you out there are already saving for your children's future college aspirations or desire to begin so you can help out your kids in some way as my parents once did. Having money saved and accessible to pay for one's college degree is life changing. As a result of earning a number of academic and merit scholarships, being a Resident Advisor (RA) on campus , and having parents who saved for me from the time I was born, student loans were not a factor. My wife had nowhere near what some people leave school with, as her parents were gracious to partially help her college tuition situation. Although, even still, she carried a hefty $50,000 of debt via Sallie Mae into our marriage. For better or for purse, I mean worse. That's how the vows go, right? We paid this college debt off as quickly as possible to cut the cost of insane interest rates and get back to ground zero.

I have a great problem with 17 or 18 year old kids signing their life away. It happens in the military and it happens with college. Don't get me wrong, both can be very good, but these teens just learned to drive and wipe their own behinds. Truly, a signature from such a young person which signs them up in a matter of seconds for a decade or more of financial commitment is preposterous. Literally, this is what is being done every year, all over the country. Over 44.7 million Americans have student loans on file, adding up to a staggering $1.56 trillion of debt as of February of 2019. That number continues to rise and there is no ceiling in sight. Why are we allowing this to happen? Let's be honest, we cannot expect that a kid fresh outta high school should know the value of money and what the loan he or she is signing up for truly means. Well, at least we should not if they haven't been greatly informed on every facet, which 99.9% are not. If people were honest and said to a young person that they were going to work for the next 10-15 years or longer just to pay off their student loans and that the total amount in many cases will have nearly doubled by the end of their debt payoff, what do you think their response would be? Do you think they would sign that dotted line? The book of Proverbs says it so well, "The rich rule over the poor, and the borrower is slave to the lender." (Proverbs 22:7). Now, you do not need to be living in the Bible belt to understand what this means people.

During my deep data dive I had the privilege of interviewing a plenty of college graduates who have completed school a number of years ago and reflected upon their experiences. One humble and transparent person who was willing to share the truth about the financial situation she faced and was completely vulnerable was a girl I met named Kat. Kat had gone to the University of Delaware and is now a very successful high school guidance counselor for inner city students. She has utilized her degree and her life to better the lives of other young people in order to help teach and guide them. Her guidance has been instrumental in ways that she did not receive as a young person herself. Being a school guidance counselor has allowed her to empower those who will be our future leaders and a big part of Kat's success has been her focus on navigating her students through the college scene with critical financial decisions. Kat reflected on a pivotal time in her own life as a student, soon after she graduated from college, that woke her up in a startling manner. In the paragraph below I invite you to listen to Kat's story. For those of you who have graduated with student loans, there are parts, like I did, where you will completely relate to Kat's message on an even deeper level. What occurred in Kat's life is extremely similar to that of hundreds of thousands of graduates who should be building their future with the degree they earned, meanwhile they are forced to try to stay afloat and not drown in student loan debt. Then, the next step these young people, who tend to not be so young when the debt is continuing to be paid off, are forced to make is to rebuild their damaged lives. At this point they are merely attempting to gain some sort of traction when at last they reach the $0 owed threshold. If you haven't gone away to college yet, or are still in a university, hopefully you will learn some important things to avoid a situation that is extremely difficult to overcome. Here is what Kat had to say.

"Once I graduated College, I had an incredible summer. I went out with friends, bought gifts, went to concerts, paid for dinners, bought new clothes, and then it happened. I checked my bank account... overdraft fee -$15.00. I could not believe it. I remember being mortified trying to scramble up dollars to pay the overdraft fee to avoid a late payment. I emptied my change cups, scoured the couch cushions to scrounge up enough to pay off the fee. I was so embarrassed, I didn't want to tell or ask anyone for help. I just knew my parents would have reprimanded me that I was foolish with my money. I somehow gathered up the money and went into the local Chase branch with a bag of coins and crumpled dollar bills. I think that was the moment, I knew I wanted to make some changes. I got a summer job as a baby photographer and then six months later, the next thing hit. Student loans....$500 per month! Again, in disbelief I scoured the letters, circling back. I didn't sign up for this? There's no way! Someone should have told me, I thought. There goes a huge piece of my earnings."

There is a better way to navigate the college ranks than to drown in student loans for decades. There is no need to have to go to a private school that costs two or three times as much as state tuition. Not to mention, the first two years of any degree are filled with pre-requisites and core classes that need to be taken in order to be set up for your major of study. All of this can be done extremely well and at a minimal cost at a community college or junior college. Nowadays with the way high school education is advancing, many kids can even take these classes for free as part of their junior or senior year and begin college with tons of credits. All of this saves big time money when pursuing that degree. In addition, there are work study jobs on campus, working off campus, and being an RA (Resident Advisor) as just a few options to help pay for tuition.

Imagine the weight that would be lifted off the shoulders of a college graduate who leaves school and that stage after receiving their diploma without the thousands and thousands of loan debt. I was fortunate to be one of these young people who had parents who helped me and was educated at a young age to understand what I would have to do to help myself. It pains me to see those smiling, excited, and enthusiastic college graduates entering the workforce, only to be crushed by Sallie Mae and other loan agencies who are charging upwards of 13% interest. Unfortunately, the situation and system is broken and needs to be fixed. What we must focus on is what we can control now. That focus must be on informing young people and shedding light on the way one can go about navigating through this college process in order to keep costs lower. It is time that our young people understand the why and the how.

Studying at a university and going away to school has great benefits. The amount of personal growth and development, maturity gained, and paving a path for one's future are all significant. And yet, debt reigns supreme in so many cases. College isn't for everyone. Wait, did he just say that? Yes, I did! I would never deter someone from desiring the acquisition of knowledge, however I would offer to steer them in a direction that would help them take a road that is not laden with extreme debt for decades to come. A degree is a degree. Whether you receive it from a state school, a private college or are an Ivy League brainiac, the world we live in now is not as impressed with that piece of paper than they are with the person in front of them. And that is how it should be. Meanwhile, college is not for everyone. In some cases it is a far worse decision to go away to school when you do not know what you want to study, aren't sure if the college is the right fit, let alone if the degree you are pursuing actually will end up providing access to a well paying career. There is something to be said in the lost art of the trades. There are great jobs and careers that pay well and require only a trade schooling that in many cases is paid for by your employer to do so many skilled professions. Starting up a small business or working in a variety of areas to figure out what you truly enjoy doing are much more cost effective ways of discerning and realizing what will be a suitable career. The notion of getting the degree or beginning work for a company and sticking it out until retirement for a 30-40 year ride is far gone. Back in 2018, the *Bureau of Labor Statistics* reported that the average person changes jobs ten to fifteen times, with an average of 12 job changes, during his or her career. It is often that many workers spend less than five years working each job. I cannot tell you how many of my friends went away to school and are paying obscene student loans back for a degree that they have not utilized in many years because they are working in a totally unrelated field. I am now a byproduct of working outside of my degree area. In fact my job has changed three times already since I graduated in 2011 with my master's degree. So whether you choose to go to college or not, I urge you to make some more informed and more sound decisions. Your finances are extremely important. Your future self will be thankful that you didn't rush into something that you later might regret or will set you back for a long time. And remember, most education doesn't come in the form of a degree. Four years away at school can teach you a lot, however, you are on a journey of becoming a lifelong learner. The more you learn about topics like money, the better!

Baby Step 5 & College Savings Options

For those of you out there who are in baby step five and desire to save for your child's college education or at least support them with what you can financially, there are some good vehicles to get into. A 529 plan is probably the most common and best option, as it is a college savings vehicle, known as a qualified tuition plan. The 529 allows you to save money for your child's college education with some great benefits. With this type of savings plan, you get to have your money that you contribute, grow without paying taxes on it at all. There are no capital gains taxes and no tax upon withdrawal as long as the money is used to pay college expenses. If your child, whose name the account was created for, decides not to go to school or receives full scholarships, the money can be used and rolled over to another child in the same family without penalty. If the money assets in your 529 are not used for something college related and you wish to access the funds other than for qualified education expenses, you can do so but there is a penalty. On top of paying federal income taxes on the 529 funds, you will also send 10% to Uncle Sam as well as a penalty on the earnings. If your scholar earns a full ride to college, the penalty for taking the cash out of the 529 account is waived. Many people use this type of savings plan, however some are now investing their money instead and gifting or paying for the tuition costs when they arrive down the road. Either way, saving is being done for your child's education which is a tremendous help that they will not realize until later on when they have less or no debt and can do so much more than their peers.

Three Tips for Young people Navigating the College Situation
(Provided by: Kat, High School Guidance Counselor)

Tip 1: **Take an interest early.** I wish as a senior in high school I really thought about my financial future and sought out resources.

Tip 2: **Learn the Debt to Income ratio.** Do a COST analysis of expected income and loan pay off. Exhaust all options, and have the college financial aid offices work with you to gain full understanding of what is the bottom line. College is a business, know the facts.

Tip 3: **You define your finances**. Take ownership of what and how you want to control your money. The choices you make link together, you can adapt and make changes.

CHALLENGE #11: *Inform a young person about student loans and start a savings fund for your child to help offset college costs.*

If you have children and are at baby step five and desire to help them with the cost of college that is great. And if you do not, no worries. The challenge is to get the information out there. Take the initiative to speak to a high school senior about their plans and let them know about what you just learned in this chapter. Think of it like going back in time and doing what maybe you wished someone would have done for you. After all, it takes a village to raise a child.

"Spend less than you make. Sounds ridiculous but many people don't really get it."

-Tom, Global Manager Cisco Systems

CHAPTER 13: Living Within Your Means

You just got that promotion and with it comes a big raise!! Woohoo! Time to celebrate. I can hear that victory music right now. Working hard and getting to the next level is important. Your inner self and the dopamine that is rushing to your brain begins to cloud your vision and you start thinking, SPEND, SPEND, SPEND! It is time to up that lifestyle, buy a more expensive vehicle, and go on a big time shopping spree for new clothes and the latest iPhone. Pump the breaks for a moment and hear me out. More money is a great thing. A higher income is awesome, most of all because if utilized responsibly it can do absolute wonders to your long term financial situation. You are now entering an even better realm than before. This newfound money means a greater ability to do bigger things with your finances and pad that portfolio. Financial freedom is a whole lot easier and comes much more quickly with more money. That goes without saying! This is all my hope for you. However, I tend to know how the story goes most of the time for people these days when it comes to landing that raise or promotion. Not so fast. You have heard it plenty of times from co-workers, family members, and neighbors, "I am now going to buy…" You fill in the blank. Unfortunately, so often the story ends by means of the saying, *more money, more problems.* America is arguably the wealthiest nation in the world and yet more people are drowning in debt. With all of this green in our nation, why are so many people working until they are halfway in the grave. We have a problem that is extensive and hurting our society vastly. Why is this? The answer, greed and a lack of satisfaction. This two headed monster is a recipe for disaster. Greed and not being satisfied with what we have often leads us down the rabbit hole of constantly wanting and claiming we need MORE! It is as if people in the United States have the mindset of a toddler embodying the persona of an undisciplined and untaught child. The negative attitude keeps Americans shouting like a little kid wearing a soggy diaper, "I want more!"

The phrase that I hear every so often, in order to justify expenses on upscaling lifestyle is, "I deserve it." Here is the thing, I am not going to be the one to sit here and tell you that you don't. I am in no position to do that, nor do I truly know how hard you had to work or hustle to get to where you are today. First of all, I commend you for earning that raise, promotion, or bonus money. Great work! However, what I do know is that if you aren't careful and get sucked into this mindset of the *MORE mentality*, it can be detrimental. Prior to the chapter we heard a quote from Tom, one of Cisco Systems Global managers who oversees numerous continents. Managing thousands of people and millions of dollars is not an indicator of responsibility, I don't know what is. Whether you make $50,000 a year or are a professional athlete and bring in tens of millions, living within or even below your means will allow you to stay far away from debt and become financially free.

Living with your means is all about continuing to not bite off more than you can chew. When people get that bonus, receive a promotion or land a new position, the dollar bills tend to blind them. The budget, if they ever had one in the first place, goes right out the window. Steak and lobster, pulling up in that hot new ride, and upgrading to an amazing house with a view. Sounds nice right? Well, honestly there is nothing wrong with it if you are able to afford it. At this point you know the program. When we say afford, we should really heed the words of best selling rapper and legend Jay Z who said, "If you can't buy it twice, you can't afford it." I like this mantra because when people are bringing in that dough, they often go crazy and get caught up in that more, more, more mentality and don't know when or how to stop.

Each of us is, but one stupid mistake away from blowing decades of hard work and that is not something that can be taken lightly. I am not advocating for living a poor man's life if you have enough money coming in and are investing wisely. However, too often people have champagne taste on a beer budget. Making more doesn't necessarily mean that you have to spend more. If you choose to do so, then it is a must to ensure that your ratio is in proportion. When we allow things to get out of whack, you will end up getting whacked up good later on and it hurts any progress we might have made for the long haul.

Most people when they get that raise, disregard the amount of debt that they have to pay off, and go straight for one upping that lifestyle. I cannot tell you how many people laughed at me for many years because I drove a modest small sedan, shopped at Aldis (low budget grocery store), hardly ever ate out, packed my lunch every single day, and chose to not go crazy with any bar tab. The list goes on and those daily lifestyle choices remain the same to this day. I actually got a nickname that I hold in high regard because of all of this. In my family and neck of the woods, I am known as "Mr. Expenditures" and at other times they call me "Mr. Discipline." I take this as the biggest compliment. The important thing to stress is that when we are wise with how we utilize more income we can allow our money to make even more for us. Why go out and spend that entire bonus? Why throw all of your increased raise into buying more stuff that you truly do not need and will only bring you fleeting happiness? A purchase here or there is good and being generous with what we have to bless others is extremely important and noble. Yet, Americans year after year and decade after decade live out the hit song by Ariana Grande entitled *7 Rings.* The line that comes to mind most of all for me is, "I see it, I like it, I want it, I got it." There is a reason why the malls continue to be packed, online shopping is at an all time high, and the economy even after a pandemic is going to be just fine. People love to spend. Imagine if they put that raise into their 401K, or invested even part of it into an index fund. Instead of spending that entire $2,000 bonus, of the extra $500 per month coming from an increase in salary, they could have invested it and turned it into tens of thousands over the course of time.

There is something to be said about a more simplistic lifestyle or at least being grateful and satisfied with what we have. The majority of people reading this book right now fall into the category of the richest 10% of the world's population. I know you might not feel rich, but you have the ability to amass some serious wealth, become financially free and have such peace if you just live within your means. Stop making the comparisons, don't worry about what others are doing or where they are at in terms of the financial game. Continue to work hard and pay attention to the basics. Keep a level head and when you make more, invest more instead of spending more.

Becoming an everyday millionaire is accessible to so many people. After reading *Everyday Millionaires* it made me understand that it doesn't matter if your salary is $200,000 or $30,000 per year. If we don't live within your means and fail to make wise decisions, all that money will go right down the drain. The tortoise and the hare was one of my all time favorite childhood fables. Growing up in the country I had the privilege of seeing a tortoise and a hare on the property my parents owned as rabbits ran wild out in those meadows and turtles came to the stream for a drink. I actually had a pet bunny and a turtle I named Pete. Therefore I nearly fell out of my chair laughing when my mom presented the book to me because no way could a turtle beat a rabbit. Impossible. But you know how the saying from the fable goes, "Slow and steady wins the race." Don't run too fast or too hard trying to live up to a standard that you cannot afford. Be a little more content about where you are at and it will do a great service to your present self and future self. This holds true when it comes to finances as well as living with an attitude of gratitude and contentment. The great Calvin Coolidge, the 30th President of the United States, led our nation to and through a time of great economic success. All the while, he personally demonstrated his dedication to preserve the old moral and economic concepts of frugality, in an era of material prosperity. This served him well, especially when the great depression began. Coolidge is known for saying, "There is no dignity quite so impressive, and no independence quite so important, as living within your means." Maintaining a standard of living that falls within the confines of one's budget and income level is extremely important. Investors can often take it to the next level when they achieve higher income and simply maintain a standard of living, as over time the cost of their standard of living will actually decrease. By not increasing the cost of living and your lifestyle so much, you can get ahead both now and for decades to come!

CHALLENGE #12 : The next time you get a raise, invest at least 50% of the money or use it to pay off debt.

Oh no! Was that another siren? Not the fun police coming down on me again and taking away all the good times! For this challenge your objective is to invest at least half of your next raise or bonus if you are debt free. For those of you still working on your debt snowball, throw as much as possible of that extra cash toward that debt. The other half if you desire, you can use to spend. Just be smart and don't take on an expense that will bleed your pockets.

"The paid-off home mortgage has taken the place of the BMW as the status symbol of choice."

-Dave Ramsey

CHAPTER 14:
Payoff Your Home Early & Other Things that Matter

Putting ourselves in the position to pay off a home early or another big ticket item is game changing to say the least. Growing up, I always wondered how my parents were able to take my brother and I on such amazing vacations, as well as help pay our college tuition bills at high cost private schools. They lived on a budget, but so did a number of the kid's parents who went to my high school. My parents lived fairly modest lives and were both teachers for the good duration of their careers. So what was it that was the magic recipe that afforded us the ability to go to far off places around the globe including Europe and Hawaii numerous times, and on average a cruise a year for over a decade? Without a shadow of a doubt it was initiating baby step six, paying off their home early that paid great benefits. The mortgage is yet another form of debt that sticks around for 30 years and is something that "everyone has to do." Wrong! Yeah, you heard me. You do not and should not pay thirty years of a mortgage, unless your tenant is footing the bill on that rental property, while you build equity.. If you desire to get ahead when you become debt free and are investing 15% into your retirement or like minded investment accounts for the future, paying your home off early is imperative. In this section we will dissect the home pay off, as well as how applying these financially savvy and winning principles can change your life forever.

At thirty years old I was living in a paid for home. Let me remind you that my wife and I busted our butts for four years to pay off our thirty year mortgage super early. He said, if you throw as much as you can at the mortgage you will put yourself years ahead of the game. Let's face it, we can all find ways to spend money that doesn't need to be spent on more stuff that won't show for anything later down the line. My dad told me a piece of very wise advice and that was to simply pay off your home early. I was the prime beneficiary of the sweat equity and sacrifices my mom and he made all those years ago. I knew that I desired to set myself up for success. The numbers are completely insane! After reading these figures below, you will not be able to disregard this idea anymore and will hopefully view your own mortgage situation much differently. Wise investors do things differently. I had a number of friends tell me, you are wrong. Instead of paying off your house early and investing the difference, you can come out way further ahead. They were wrong. Not to mention there is a guarantee when paying off your house early, you then own that and it is a complete asset in your portfolio. When the crisis of a pandemic strikes, you are laid off, you do not have to worry because you will have a roof over your head. This might not be the most convincing part of the argument you say. Well, the numbers when we break them down in a bit will be every bit the necessary evidence to paint the clearest picture possible.   This strategy really works.

It was the spring of 2015 and I had just moved into my home in upstate, NY. Having purchased the property, a nice three bedroom, 1,500+ square foot home with two full baths and a modern updated interior for $182,500.   I was excited. My wife would be moving in after we got married in a few months. Soon we would set off on the best part of our life together. The mortgage back then, including the taxes and insurance escrowed came in at $1,050 a month. Most people who sign a 30 year loan at 4.125% interest would make that monthly payment for three decades and then own their home. If you haven't learned this about me yet, this section will accentuate it all the more, I hate debt! After paying 20% down on this house initially, we would still owe a base of $146,000. That is a serious chunk of change. This did not sit well with me. However, when I started the number crunching I refused to allow this to be the case because what I found out was startling.

My $182,500 home which I enjoyed living in back then and still appreciate to this day, was on my mind continuously. I knew that I had to do something about the payments. I figured out that if I were to go the duration of the loan, my wife and I would be paying out on average approximately $5,000 every year in interest alone over a thirty year period. That is roughly $150,000 in mere interest. Disturbing, I know! Keep in mind that $150K or $5K per year doesn't account for a single penny off the principal premium. Wow, that's a ton of money that wouldn't be working in my favor for decades.   My next step was to access a mortgage amortization chart. This tool outlines the loan payoff and how much can be saved when extra payment amounts are made. By seeing the payment schedule on my loan, I could visualize how much money I could save if I made even one extra full payment on my mortgage every year. The first adjustment that I made was calling up PennyMac Loan Services and putting into place bi-weekly payments on my mortgage. So instead of paying my mortgage in full once a month, I would begin paying out half the mortgage amount every two weeks. Over the course of the year, one extra payment would be made based on the payout bi-weekly schedule. As a result I learned that this single choice alone would save my wife and I nearly seven years of payments on our home! I trimmed down my 30 year mortgage and turned it into a 23 year term, just like that. Not too bad, I must say! If you do nothing else, at least take advantage of the bi-weekly payment. But then I read that the average everyday millionaire pays off their home in 10.1 years. 23 years is a far cry from 10. How would I be able to make up such substantial ground? Certainly, the answer was rebalancing my budget and making more money. Increasing my income and my wife stepping up her game would be a golden ticket to helping us pay off our home earlier.

For me the numbers were enough to be motivated to install a new payment program and align our budget to throw every dollar, literally every dollar extra toward our mortgage. It took a bit more convincing for my better half to get on board, but she did. For us, this meant some serious changes. Looking at owing $296,000 on top of the nearly $40,000 we had already paid out for the downpayment and closing costs seemed insane to me on a house that had a value in 2015 of around $180K. One word kept flashing in my mind over and over, DUMB! I did not want to be a slave to my home and the mortgage lender for three decades. I wanted to take a winning approach. After a detailed conversation and explaining everything to my wife, we made the best decision of our financial lives and started crushing the mortgage. In the prime of our mortgage payoff during that four year period, there was a stretch of approximately 20-24 months or so where we poured $5,500 per month toward the principal balance of our home. Doing so, literally took us down to the last penny in our account each month. I know what you are thinking, this guy is crazy! Well, for us it was crazier to lose out on all that cash doing wonders for us down the line. Who pays off 5X their minimum mortgage payment each month? I am willing to bet less than 1% of the population. I mention all of this to you, not to brag, but to inform. Great gains happen when you make some serious sacrifices. It was not only dumping all of our cash into the home being paid off, it was countless months of not eating out, buying literally nothing we wanted, and saying no to just about everything. You might not be as driven as I was and you don't have to be as strict, but the harder you push, the more results you will see. Whether you can pay off your home in 48 months like we did, in a decade, or in twenty years, no matter how much sooner it is before the 30 year loan maturity, it will save you tons of money by paying it off early! That is the key, pay off your home early. I love to tap into the best fighter of all time, Muhammad Ali when times get tough. No one was better than *The Champ* and it was mostly because no one else was willing to do what Ali would do to prepare and train. The float like a butterfly and sting like a bee mentality in the ring is one thing on fight night. Waking up at 4am, running, lifting, jumping rope, and pushing your body to the absolute max is another. Ali's words keep me grounded and with a heavy weight fighter's mentality when attacking our mortgage as the great one reminded me of his strive for greatness, "I hated every minute of training, but I said, 'Don't quit. Suffer now and live the rest of your life as a champion.'" It was all about sacrifice and not throwing in the towel. We made it and now are living in our paid off home like champs!

The home I now wake up in everyday and the driveway I pull into after work each evening feels unbelievably different. My wife and I truly own our home. What is even more exciting for me though is how we can utilize that money we saved in interest that would have otherwise been paid out to PennyMac, our mortgage lender, for decades and decades to come. 2045 is a very long time from now. So how can we maximize the money we saved in interest payments and use it for our good? The possibilities are endless. After doing detailed math, I figured out that we paid a shade over $20,000 in interest in the four years we had a mortgage. As much as I hate this amount, I love the next one all the more. The $130,000 we saved is the key! I had to reward my wife with a big time vacation to Europe where we went away for two weeks to London, Paris, the Amalfi Coast in Italy, and Greece. It was amazing. An $8,000 vacation was affordable because we had a paid off home and no mortgage to deal with. This is an example of rewarding yourself for a big time goal being met.

Since paying off our home early, my focus has been on two things, investing more in the market, namely in stocks and index funds, as well as getting more involved in real estate. Knowing how much compound interest can benefit someone, let's have some fun and play with this $130,000 amount saved on interest payments from tackling our home mortgage early. So obviously the $130K is not a lump sum that we have in our bank account right now from paying off the house early. However, the extra $5,000 per year in interest alone we do have, as well as not being tied to a $1,050 mortgage payment, which equates to another $7,000 per year after taxes and homeowners insurance. Combining $7K and $5K in interest not having to be paid, essentially frees up an additional $12,000 per year for us. Even taking simply the interest alone, the $5,000 saved by kicking PennyMac to the curb, we would net $637,622.50 based on the S&Ps 9.8% return over the next 26 years of being mortgage free by investing the interest money exclusively. By not having the minimum house payment, we also can invest that extra $7,000 per year at a similar rate and that can turn into another $892,671.50. Added up, those amounts combined total a staggering $1,530,294. Yes, you heard me. We not only saved $130,000 in interest payments alone, but flipped the script on our financial future by freeing up that money, which we would have otherwise paid out in interest over a 30 year loan. In doing so we now have the potential to leverage that cash and make a $1.5 million gain by investing it soundly over the next two and a half decades. If that doesn't excite someone, I am not sure what will.

So maybe you are thinking to yourself, based on my minimum mortgage payment and my household income situation, it is not feasible to pay it off in four years. No problem. What if you paid it off in fifteen years, half the amount of time as the thirty year term or you really got serious and did it in ten? The hundreds of thousands you will save in interest is enough alone to make this decision. Knowing what your extra freed up money will be able to turn into in the long run is even more convincing of a factor. This will not be easy and there will be moments that you are asking yourself, why? If your why is big enough, the numbers don't lie and speak volumes, then you can do pretty much anything. The *reason* for my wife and I was to be able to pay for that dream home down the line in cash so that we don't have to ever worry about a mortgage or debt again. Another big part of our *why* was so that we could bless other people and travel around the world making memories with those we love. Whatever your why is, it must be solidified, otherwise you will jump off the horse and stop riding along the way. There were moments during the four years that my wife adamantly articulated that she did not want to continue to pay off the house at the rate we were doing so. "I hate this." "When will this ever be over?" Discipline and doing things in an uncommon fashion is never easy nor is it comfortable. We endured and we powered through. Now we are reaping the rewards in the present and have lots of great options in our future as we are becoming more and more financially free.

Mortgages 101: 15 Year vs. 30 Year Fixed

In the world of mortgages, the two most common options that are utilized and that I would recommend are the conventional 15 year or 30 year fixed rate options. Sure there are a plethora of others out there worth noting, including and not limited to:

- Interest-Only Mortgage
- Adjustable Rate Mortgage (ARM)
- FHA Loans
- VA Loans
- Combo / Piggyback
- Balloon
- Jumbo

Since the nature of this book is to be a comprehensive guide, I am not going to dissect each of these. I encourage you to pick up one of Dave Ramsey's books or another mortgage heavy text to get into the nitty gritty. There is great value and importance to just see how much of a difference paying off your home in half the time can be. Let's take a look at what Chloe ran into when deciding which conventional fixed rate mortgage would be better for her financial situation. Chloe needed to borrow $250,000 as that was her loan amount. On a 15 year mortgage, she learned that she would have a lower interest rate at 3.6% and be making 180 total payments, half of that of a 30 year term. Her monthly payment broke down to $1,745 which she could certainly afford based on her budget. Meanwhile, she will have paid $60,195 in interest in the 15 years and a total amount paid of $260,195. If Chloe were to go with the 30 year loan, the interest rate would be nearly ¾ of a percent higher, while her monthly payment would be much lower at $1,293. This frees up almost $500 per month for her budget. The drastic difference is that a 30 year loan will lead Chloe to pay a colossal $157,577 in interest and $357,577 in total! So being the wise investor and smart financial decision maker she is, she decides to take the 15 year option. This saves Chloe nearly $100,000 by simply taking the 15 year option as opposed to the 30 year loan. See the graphic below which can help you understand the tale of the tape comparing the two loan lengths side by side.

	Loan Amount $250,000	
15-Year		**30-Year**
180	Number of Payments	360
3.6%	Average Interest Rate	4.3%
$1,745	Monthly Payment	$1,293
$60,195	Total Interest Paid	$157,577
$260,195	Total Amount Paid	$357,577

That's over $97,000 in savings with a 15-year fixed-rate mortgage!

The principles and strategies that you have learned in this section of paying off a mortgage early can be applied to basically any and every loan that you have. The thing is, the higher the interest rate your loan is set at, the more money you will save by paying off that loan early. Making minimum payments to college student loans at 8-12% interest is devastating because the principal isn't the big cost, but that interest. That is why the hamster wheel keeps spinning round and round and it seems like no progress is being made. It is extremely important to clearly state to the lender that you want to pay off the principal with the additional funds, whether it be for a college loan, home, car, or another expense. The final thing I will say is that I sometimes hear people tell me that there are times when the debt can work in your favor. People say, but you can write off the interest you paid on your taxes. Although true, no one is getting a tax break in the amount of saving $130,000 over the next couple decades. I can promise you that. The argument about debt also comes in especially in terms of a car loan. Dan, if I can get a car loan at 2.5% or less, why would I not take that deal when I can invest money at a rate of 9.8% according to the S&P 500? See, I know that 9.8% is much higher than 2.5% and that there is a 7.3% difference between the two. What I also know is that most people are not taking any extra money and investing it to gain that 7.3% profit, not to mention that there is no complete guarantee that your investment yields returns at that rate. What is a 100% guarantee however is that the 2.5% interest you will owe for the 36 month car loan will have to be paid every month until the loan comes to completion. What I do know is that you will pay out that $130,000 in interest or $5,000 a year like I did on my home mortgage. All of that is guaranteed and if you make a late payment, there will be extra charges piled up on top of that debt as well. Leveraging debt can be a good tactic at times, especially when you get to a certain level as an investor and you completely understand concepts such as risk tolerance, taking advantage of the tax situation, and other next level financial concepts. For the everyday person, far more is gained by establishing a habit of avoiding debt, paying off loans early, and living free.

Unleash the shackles, free yourself and be a slave to debt and negative interest no more! Flip that son of a gun on its head and be the one to make the money by utilizing interest dividends in your favor. When was the last time that you heard of someone writing a book on finances that was reputable and continued to incur debt? As for me and my house as well as those I advise, we will cut out debt. It is time for us to run a different race that has proven to get much different and better results.

CHALLENGE #13: Pay off your home or loan early.

Whether it is a mortgage or is a car loan or some other expense you borrowed for, pay it off early. Lucky number thirteen challenge is to crunch some numbers and make a new goal for paying off your loan. Create a payoff plan that allows you to crush that interest and own outright whatever you borrowed for. Your stress will decrease and your pockets will fill with money because like Dave Ramsey says, "Debt is dumb and cash is king. The paid off mortgage is taking the place of the BMW as the status symbol of choice."

"Money grows on the tree of persistence."

-Japanese Proverb

CHAPTER 15:
Baby Step 7 & Living in Financial Freedom

The final baby step, baby step 7 is to get to the point where you are truly financially free. At this point in the financial journey, you can live the life you desire, as well as give generously. You are building up a legacy to pass on to your children and your children's children. You are able to take full advantage of the retirement accounts you stowed a sizable nest egg for all of those years. Those golden eggs are hatched and you are the beneficiary of hard work and discipline. For many people this will mean the ability to take those amazing trips they have looked forward to. It can mean living seasonally in warmer locations in a second home to escape the cold and being able to bless others in tremendous ways. Whatever you decide, the key here is that it is your choice! No longer do you have to go to work, but if you wanted to, you could do whatever it is that makes you most happy. Money is your friend and you have a lot of it. There is more than enough in your accounts to allow you to provide for your household, live comfortably, and enjoy spoiling those grandchildren. What if it didn't take you to reach your 60s to get to financial freedom and total financial independence?

It too often saddens me to see many people work so hard, save, invest, and do things the right way for years upon years only to miss out on their retirement. I have seen this in my own family and amongst friends and it is heart wrenching. There are no guarantees in life, besides taxes and death. Unfortunately, the latter can creep up on us when we least expect it. No one has a crystal ball and can predict the future. Although we do not know how much time we have here on earth, we can make the most of the time that we do have. Earlier on, I mentioned rewarding your progress along the way of this financial journey. I wanted to take a minute to remind you of the importance of this. Again, this is two fold. First of all, it keeps you motivated and willing to stay disciplined as there is an incremental reward along the way when you reach your goals. Second, it allows you to enjoy the journey and not be all work and no play. Building memories, having fun, and enjoying moments with those you love is extremely important. Putting all of our eggs in the retirement basket is not wise. Nor is putting all of the stake of our lives in banking on living when we get there good to do either. We must plan for it, but I am a fan of creating a different future that allows us to live out our retirement far before we get to the typical or average retirement age.

The concept and movement that is gaining in popularity is called FIRE. FIRE is an acronym that stands for Financially Independent Retire Early. If someone had a magic potion you could drink and you could remain the same age you are now and not have to work ever again, would you take that sip? I would. Not having to go to work frees us up to do what we love and spend time with the people who matter most to us. That is real independence. The FIRE community has developed a way for this to take place. In various books like the aforementioned *Choose FI* and *Playing with FIRE*, the leaders in this new wave of saving and investing help us to understand that retirement doesn't have to be some far off dream or fantasy that we might never reach. Chris Hogan in his book *Retired Inspired* when speaking of retirement is famous for saying, "It is not about an age, but about a number." It pained me to see a family member work for forty years, get sick and never be able to travel, enjoy the money that was stowed away, or live the retired life they had labored for. Becoming financially independent is all about having enough money invested that will yield a revenue stream from interest that will afford your cost of living. Typically this is done by saving and investing up to 25X your annual expenses. Once you reach that total amount you will have enough to maintain that lifestyle and account for inflation by withdrawing 4% or so annually and can be truly financially free. Let's unpack this and explain what the *4% rule* means so it is a bit easier to grasp.

4% Rule

As we know, Chloe has been doing exceptionally well at XCompany. She has made so many wise financial decisions along the way and her portfolio is becoming quite immense as the years go on. Being the wise investor that she is, Chloe realizes that she doesn't want to wait until the age of 59.5 to retire and desires to achieve financial independence, namely FI much sooner. She sat down with her husband recently and they crunched the numbers. The *4% rule* says that you can withdraw 4% of your portfolio value each year without incurring a substantial risk of running out of money. Their yearly expenses come in at around $30,000. Paying off their home, remaining debt free, and continuing to save was huge in order to cut down that total amount. In order for Chloe and her husband to reach FI and live off of their non-retirement funds, she and her husband will have to save and accrue about $750,000. This would allow them to live off of the interest and withdraw 4% of that $750,000 per year, which is $30,000 and they would never run out of money! Now you and Chloe are probably wondering how long will it take to save and invest to get to the point where one has $750,000? The FI community pledges itself on saving at least 50-70% or more of their total income monthly. This approach has led to thousands of people to be able to achieve FI in 15 years, 10 years, and sometimes even less. People who do so are able to be totally financially free and can stop work completely at the age of 50, 45, 40, and in some rare cases their 30s. The good news for Chloe and hopefully for you, is that because she and her husband have been conscientious and wise investors they are not starting at $0 today trying to hit that $750K mark. They actually don't have to hit that total amount right now at all. What? You mean it is easier? Yes, it absolutely is.

Bridging the Gap to Retirement

Truthfully, Chloe and others who want to reach financial independence and stop working must have a different number, much lower to reach FI since they already have a retirement account growing. Chloe would need the $30,000 per year of expenses X however many years is left until she turns 59.5 years old, to be saved/invested. At this point, Chloe is 45 and she desires to stop working at 50. By the time she is 50 years old she will need to have 9.5 years (59.5-50=9.5) saved and invested to bridge the gap to get her to her retirement funds. In essence this would mean at $30K per year, she would need about $300K or so to be able to float her until she can collect on her 401K or Roth IRA accounts. In essence, that would mean saving around $30,000. That is a good amount of money, however it is possible but will take some real effort. The positive is that the total amount she needs to bridge the gap to retirement is 1.5X less than that $750,000 amount we saw earlier. The good news is that Chloe is more than half-way there and she continues to be the beneficiary of compound interest. What she decides to do is dial back her retirement contributions at this point. Instead of putting the 15% in her 401K and IRA (combo), she takes the employer match of 6% by investing 6% and takes minimally the other 9% if not more, up to the total amount she can afford to do so, and saves it. Really, this means she is investing that extra money in those index funds and stock/bond areas she already had a sizable amount in. That way, she can reach her goal, while maintaining her lifestyle. Chloe might even choose to purchase another rental property to gain access to more cash flow. Below you will find the seven steps to achieving FIRE (Financial Independence Retire Early) according to author and movement enthusiast, Scott Rieckens. From reading his book *Playing With FIRE* I have concluded that Rieckens claims that making purchases and the lifestyle we choose to lead really comes down to one recurring major question, "Is this purchase more valuable than my independence?" As you could probably guess, in short, the answer is most often, no! Some would argue an extreme vantage point, however when making large purchases it can come in handy.

THE 7 STEPS TO FIRE
1) Calculate how much you have
    - net worth=all assets minus debts
2). Figure out how much you were spending and saving
3) Reduce daily expenses
    - evaluate budget, make adjustments and sacrifice
4) Reduce the big three: housing, transportation, food
    - buy used and & stick to the budget
5) Make your savings work for you
    - index funds and real-estate investments...max out your interest rate %
6) Increase your income
    - extra income=reaching FIRE faster
7) Find a FIRE community

Certainly, financial freedom can be reached and we can retire way earlier than the norm, but it all boils down to choice and sacrifice. How you live today is going to greatly impact the way that you are able to live later on down the road. In addition, the choices you make with money that take advantage of compound interest and time by getting in the game so to speak earlier, will open up opportunities to reach FI. This will allow one to be able to step down from that 9-5 all consuming job, to work part time, or not have to work at all. As for me that is something that is super attractive. But there is only one way to reach that situation and it involves much less luck and much more hard work and dedication. Make your own luck by being disciplined and financially savvy. Live on a budget and decide not to up the standard of living every time you get that raise or bonus. Continue to invest in sound vehicles and stay out of debt. The choice is yours. You might like being able to sit on a beach ten years earlier than most people, or traveling the globe when you are young and healthy. Or perhaps it is enjoying every moment of your kids teenage years and your grandchildren from the time they are born. No matter what your fancy is, you can take time back by becoming financially independent. There is a reason why they called it *Choose FI*. Choose wisely and know that financial freedom is worked toward by taking one baby step at a time. This is a systematic approach taken day by day. I laughed many years ago when a friend of mine who owns a landscaping company said, "I am going to retire by the time I am 40." At the time we were only 20. Just the thought of that sounds very appealing to me as I am less than a decade away from reaching such an age. What I do know for certain is that life is far too short not to enjoy time and the resources we have. Achieving FI is a sure way to maximize both time and your money!

CHALLENGE #15: Crunch some numbers and see how you could reach FI

This challenge is one that really is exciting. For many people reading this book they probably haven't even heard of FI. So what I want you to do is to calculate how much money it takes to live annually. Then, take that total amount and multiple it by 25. When you get that figure, you have your FI ballpark number. How many years prior to turning 59.5 would you want to stop working? Subtract your age you desire to stop working at from 59.5 and that gives you how many years you have to bridge the gap of your retirement funds. Multiply the gap number by your annual expenses and this will give you the total amount you would need to save by making wise investments to reach FI. If you haven't begun a retirement account or have very little in there you would need to account for the full FI amount which is 25-30X your annual expenses to reach FI.

"If we command our wealth, we shall be rich and free. If our wealth commands us, we are poor indeed."

– Edmund Burke

CHAPTER 16:
Become an Everyday Millionaire

"At least eighty percent of millionaires are self-made. That is, they started with nothing but ambition and energy, the same way most of us start."

– Brian Tracy

Growing up in the 1990s I remember vividly the hit television show *Who Wants to be a Millionaire*. Every week host star, Regis Philbin, would excite the crowd as people answered questions across a variety of categories. As the show went on in each episode, the contestant was challenged with high level questions with the degree of difficulty always increasing. As a ten year old when that show came out, I recall being able to correctly answer all of the questions up to a $2,000 mark many times. It was really neat that each contestant also received three life lines including ask the audience, 50/50, and my personal favorite, phone a friend. These lifelines would allow a contestant to receive help on puzzling questions in hopes of correctly answering each and then moving on to the next round. In order to win the cool million dollar total prize pot, 14 questions would have to be answered correctly in a thirty minute time span. The phrase, Is that your final answer became ever so popular during this show as well. There were a number of times where contestants would walk away with the money they had earned up to that point and I remember a few times where people ran the table taking home the entire $1,000,000.

As a kid, who wouldn't want to be rich and become a millionaire. That same mentality goes for all of us. The number one million seemed so distant and untouchable. The only way I thought one could get there was by winning the lottery, which required a ton of luck. Don't hold your breath, your odds of winning the Mega Millions Jackpot are 1 in 302.6 million. Slim to say the least. Sorry folks, but it is not going to happen. However, becoming an everyday millionaire is obtainable and I began to believe that in my 20s after reading Chris Hogan's book *Everyday Millionaire: How Ordinary People Built Extraordinary Wealth & How You Can Too.* The very title captivated my attention. I don't normally judge a book by it's cover, and yet this cover was intriguing. Was it really possible to become a millionaire? As a little boy, I remember my dad saying to us that we would have to work hard and save. He mentioned numerous times that if we were fortunate we would make possibly a million dollars for all of our jobs and salaries during our working career combined. At the time, even as a kid, I had enough common sense to know that everything costs money. So that meant that there was no real way we were going to become a millionaire. This was unless of course we won the lotto, became a professional athlete, or someone we knew was wealthy and gave us a pile of money.

The dream of becoming a millionaire was dead, over, and gone forever. Until it was not. Reading Hogan's book resurrected the feasibility that everyday people like you and like me could actually become millionaires. I had not realized that there was a blueprint that made achieving this milestone status actually obtainable. I found out that the recipe for becoming a millionaire was a lot more simply than I had originally thought. The best part was that it didn't require any luck at all. It all came down to a few simple principles: becoming debt free and staying that way, living on a budget, saving, and investing. Well, the good news for us is that we have discussed at length each of these areas. When you put them all in the same financial crockpot, over the long haul that calls for a sweet sweet recipe. Success will begin chasing you down and you will be on your way toward becoming most likely the first millionaire in your family. If you desire this, great! It is time for you to make it your reality.

There is literally nothing that can stop you from becoming a millionaire, besides you. No one can tell you what to do with your money. Well, I guess they can, but you don't have to listen to the negative or naysayers. After all, you are the one rising and grinding every day and making the bread as they used to say back in the good old days. Keep making hay when the sun is shining and stick to the principles we outlined in this book. See, becoming an everyday millionaire based on a regular workers salary is not about striking it big and getting rich quick. No, it is all about the process. Back to the tortoise and the hare. Slow and steady will win the race and it is really encouraging to know that there are a ton of everyday millionaires. I do like being different. In fact, I pride myself on being uncommon. Standing alone and sticking out from the rest of the pack is a good thing. Differentiating what I do when compared to the norm is something that I abide by. However, it does make it more attainable and it does make it more feasible to reach millionaire status knowing that there are nearly 19 million millionaires in our country alone and nearly 50 million millionaires in the world. Let's look at that U.S. statistic a bit more and examine it further. Of the 209 million adults in the U.S, 19 million are millionaires or about 9% of the adult population in this country. I can definitely roll with that. One out of every 11 people becomes a millionaire, to me that is a very good probability. No chance, luck, or fortune has to come your way. The coolest thing is that literally everyone has the ability to make their millionaire dream a reality.

Accumulating and building a net worth of a million dollars happens over time. The more money we make and the less we spend, the faster this process can be accelerated. Income is a huge factor, but what we do with that income is even more important. One of my favorite stories in the *Everyday Millionaire* book is about a janitor. Making an average salary of $30,000 over the duration of his career, he was able to amass a net worth of a million dollars in about 35 years. Three and a half decades of hard work, determination, focus, intentionality, smart decision making, saving and investing turned a $30,000 salary into a million dollar nest egg. Cleaning and maintaining the school campus probably never felt so good for that gentleman. Having begun the career at age 22, he was sitting on a pile of cash and net worth that was seven figures by the time he was 57 years old. Imagine what you can do with your salary. If you are making $40K per year. Or how about the others out there that are bringing in $50K. I cannot even imagine what living out these principles and applying these concrete strategies can do for those of you who already are close to or at a six digit annual income. People, get with me. You should be waking up everyday and look yourself in the mirror and say, it is time to make some money and it is time to take one step closer to becoming a millionaire.

I love success stories. It makes me excited to hear stories of hard working people who build their finances from the ground up over the years. In order to reach this level of wealth, you have to have a different kind of mindset. As is the case in life, so it also falls true when it comes to money. Your mind is your greatest weapon. Your brain is either going to be owned by you and therefore become your greatest ally or you will be owned by it and your pockets will be empty. What do you want your story to be? There is no story in my opinion that is better and more powerful when it comes to having the millionaire mentality than that of actor Jim Carrey. Those of you who are in my generation or have an appreciation for humorous films know that Jim Carey is famous for his lead roles in movies like *Ace Ventura, The Mask, Liar Liar, Yes Man, Bruce Almighty, The*

Grinch, and my personal favorite, *Dumb & Dumber*. This star actor was not always a star and early on in his acting career when times were tough, well before he was rolling in the dough and made a name for himself, Carrey made a decision. Way back in 1985, some 35 years ago Carrey made an audacious decision. He woke up one morning and decided to write himself a $10-million check for "acting services rendered." On that check, he dated it for 10 years into the future. Carrey would keep that check in his wallet over the next decade. He would pull it out and look at it often. Some people would call this a strange coincidence, others luck, but in November of the year 1995, Carrey found out that he was going to be a star in the movie *Dumb and Dumber*. The $17 million budgeted film would pay Jim Carrey prodigious sum of $10 million for his lead role! How about them apples. Or should I say, how about them dollars!!

So let this be a small lesson in the power of positivity, intentionality, and chasing down your goals. Or you can become dumb or even dumber, pun fully intended, and waste away the income that you work so hard for. It is an easy choice to make, one that doesn't take much at all to begin. Your key to success is within you already. The question is what is it that is holding you back from becoming a millionaire. Like the Jay-Z billboards chart song *99 Problems* goes...you might have 99 problems, but don't allow money to be one. In most cases with a million dollars in net worth or beyond many of your problems will disappear.

Keep your foot on the gas pedal and your eyes locked on the prize. Keep looking through the windshield as you drive along the road paved to financial success. There is a reason why the windshield is a whole lot bigger than the rearview mirror. Don't focus on the setbacks or the mistakes you made along the way. It is good to learn from them, but move on. Stay fixated on the process and when you wake up those investments and fiscally sound decisions you will have made during the course of your journey by driving those savvy financial vehicles will allow you to cross the finish line as a millionaire. Let that be my *Final Answer* and may it be yours as well!

CHALLENGE 16: *Set the course of becoming an Everyday Millionaire.*

Stop buying lotto tickets and start making your own luck. Believe that it is actually possible and understand that there are millions of millionaires in this country alone and hundreds of thousands of people just like you who are choosing to live differently. As a result they are growing their net worth and systematically, slowly, but surely, becoming millionaires. Just like you created a budget, similar to creating an investment plan or retirement strategy, the same can be done to achieve a seven digit net worth. Keep in mind your net worth of a million dollars consists of all of your assets including your home, vehicles, savings, investments, and retirement accounts. I can nearly think of a million reasons you should take this challenge seriously, just get started and begin one dollar bill at a time!

"The very nature of finance is that it cannot be profitable unless it is significantly leveraged... and as long as there is debt..."

-Alan Greenspan

CHAPTER 17: Good Debt vs. Bad Debt

Throughout the duration of this book, the program we have discussed involved avoiding debt at all costs. Here we will take a look at the times when debt might indeed be necessary and when leveraged correctly can actually benefit the investor. In essence it is the notion that sometimes by taking one step backward we are able to take two giant leaps ahead. In no way am I commended or encouraging you to go into debt. However, for those who have tremendous control over their finances are in the world of business and understand the process, there is something that is called good debt. It is weird to say those two words in the same sentence, let alone the same breath, but debt can be used to benefit financial decisions. Let's take a look below at what constitutes something as being good versus bad debt.

At this stage in the game bad debt is pretty clear. When we fall behind payments, make stupid purchases, take out loans that have exuberant interest costs, or are tied down to an expense for a long period of time and become slave to it. Those are all examples of bad debt. Most investors would suggest that things like home equity loans are usually considered good debt because their interest rates are lower than other kinds of debt, like auto loans or credit cards. Bad debt is usually constituted as debt incurred to purchase things that tend to lose their value quickly and which do not generate any source of long-term income. As financial guru Robert Kiyosaki put it, "Bad debt is debt that makes you poorer." He continued to articulate the difference between bad debt and good debt by stating the following, "I count the mortgage on my home as bad debt, because I'm the one paying on it. Other forms of bad debt are car payments, credit card balances, or other consumer loans." Therefore, investments that cause short term debt that have value and pay out an income, the most common being a real estate property, is one to leverage and capitalize on. I fully endorse people who are debt free with a paid off home and have ample funds in their retirement account to go into some short term debt in order to purchase a sound piece of real estate. In the long run, the tax savings and debt that is leveraged to gain equity will turn into a big time profit. This is a plan to take advantage of in the most responsible way possible.

There are straight out bad deals and bad debt. However, there are some avenues of debt that can be utilized to maximize gains. Some of the good forms of debt include:

- Taking out a Mortgage on a rental property.
- Getting a Home Equity Loan or Line of Credit.
- Small Business Loans
- Payday Loans
- Low interest automobile loans near 0% financing

Of the so-called good debt, I am a fan of the rental property and home equity line of credit if your house is paid off in full. Business loans to start out your small business can also lead to great dividends in the future so long as the plan pans out. At times in life we need to take risks, yet mitigating that risk is crucial. Needless to say, if you don't need to take out a loan and can cash flow that real estate property, do it. Guarantees in life are few and far between. When we don't owe anyone any money we are not tied down and have the greatest freedom. Even so called good debt turns to bad debt when we have an issue or a problem arises and face trouble paying off the loan.

When we are well informed and understand how to leverage debt and use it in our favor it can be profitable. This again most often happens with real estate. Some ways that debt can make you wealthier in the long run include using it to exponentially multiply your returns. When it comes to debt leverage, this is money you are using or have borrowed to increase your return on an investment that you made. If the loan you took out is less than the investment you put the money into, you have then successfully leveraged debt and used it in your favor to make a profit and "beat the system." Leverage can allow an investor to achieve returns that would not have been possible due to a lack of cash available at the time of the investment. Still, there is a greater risk of losing one's capital by incurring the debt even during times of leverage as a result of a lack of guarantee on the investment.

Exploring Debt Leverage

An example of debt leverage looks like this. Chloe decides to get heavily involved in real estate and is now looking to flip houses to make a sizable profit. She understands that she doesn't have the capital at the moment to purchase the foreclosure property outright, so she takes out a home equity line of credit. This allows Chloe to leverage the money or equity that is in her house to purchase the additional property. She will have to pay this home equity loan back at a much lower rate than the profit margin she will make by turning the foreclosure into a nice home through modernization and renovations. The $60,000 she borrowed from herself, essentially, becomes a net profit of $50,000 as she sells the newly renovated and once condemned property she accessed for very cheap having turned it into a big time profit. That is a way to leverage debt. One other non real estate example would be when you can get an auto loan for 2.0% and meanwhile you are investing money at 9-10% in an index fund. By paying the minimum monthly payment and interest on the car loan, you can net 7-8% using debt leveraged to make money instead of using the cash that is earning the higher interest rate. This actually flips debt in your favor. Finally, credit card balances paid off each month in full are in a sense debt also. They are always considered bad debt when not paid on time and in full. However, if you continue to stick strictly to your monthly budget and pay your one credit card off every month on time, you can leverage debt by borrowing the money in the short term and earn nice cash back bonuses or travel miles. Again, I only advise having a credit card once you are debt free and are financially disciplined enough to not only pay the entire balance off each month, but to not spend more because you are living on that budget. However, when it comes to the basics of achieving financial peace, I still like saving up for the car and cash flowing monthly expenses instead of using the credit card, to ensure you stay on the path to freedom. The debt leveraged when used correctly with real estate can be extremely profitable and is one for advanced investors to take full advantage of.

CHALLENGE #17: Examine Your Debt

If you are going to try to leverage debt, know what you are doing and also evaluate the situation well beforehand. Only utilize debt when you have an ample plan in place and are already personally debt free with a paid off home. Borrowing money for a real estate investment for a second home to use as a rental property is a strategic move to grow passive income streams and build net worth, including equity over time. This is about the only debt that I believe is good.

"To build a successful business, you must start small and dream big."

-Alika Dagnote

CHAPTER 18: Building a Small Business

Ambition, hard work, dedication, and relentlessness are all qualities of successful small business owners. I have nothing but great respect for people who pour their time and energy into an idea and business that they believe in. Building a business is hard, but it can be a way to capitalize on a specific market and grow wealth, as well as both passive and active income streams. With the hustle and the hard work comes risk of failure. But in order to achieve it, you must believe in it as well as be willing to do whatever it takes to see it through!

According to the U.S. Bureau of Labor Statistics, this coming pre Coronavirus times, information on small business failure was quite alarming. The rate reported and published was over 20% of all small businesses fail within their first year of existence. To make matters worse for those who aspire to run and operate a small business, roughly 33% of small businesses fold within just two years. So why get caught up in something that has a 1 in 3 chance of flopping? Well, the people who go after achieving something important are typically the ones that want it bad enough to make it work. As the saying goes, where there is a will, there is a way. Unless of course there is no money left, then there is no longer a way.

Let's take some time to explore the good, the bad, the pros, the cons, the lovely, and the ugly when it comes to owning and operating a small business. I personally do not own a small business, however I do work for one, I have in-laws who operate them, and a slew of relatives who have done so over the course of my lifetime. Starting out in the small business world is so challenging for a number of reasons. The costs associated with getting up and running are often quite vast with no guarantee return. From the onset it is all risk and no sight of reward. However, the words of Richard Branson can be encouraging. They are short and sweet, yet pack a powerful punch. Branson said, "A big business starts small." He is so right. The Megatron businesses that are seemingly running the world were once tiny startup companies. The best example of this is Amazon, as Jeff Bezos began his distribution company way back in the mid 1990s in his garage. His business soon became known as the world's largest book distributor at the time. The rest, well as you know, is history. Now we aren't going to focus on the likes of Jeff Bezos, Bill Gates of Microsoft, or

Steve Jobs of Apple. I don't know them, although like most wise investors, I do own shares of each of those large cap companies.

My first personal experiences with small businesses came by means of my aunt and uncle who owned a local ice cream shop in my small hometown of Germantown, NY, as well as my great uncle who owned a gun shop and realty outfitter. The ice cream parlor was a little seasonal side hustle to stay engaged in the community and provide for a way to bring people together. From my observance and understanding, it was anything but a money making machine. The gun shop and most definitely the realty business were two that thrived, the latter which is still running strong today. My uncle Ralph had some great success as a businessman largely due to his personality and his understanding of how to manage money. Hard to believe right? Well, these three aspects are often what give an extreme edge to a small business owner. Couple this with great organizational skills and a drive to get through whatever comes your way, and you will be successful.

After meeting my now wife, I soon became aware that her parents both had small business which they built from the ground up. Not only that, they have operated them successfully for the past 40 years. For me this was incredible to hear. The one run by my now mother-in-law called Cachet, is a hair salon, while my father-in-law has a carpet cleaning and emergency restoration business entitled SuperClean. Although their businesses are totally different, they have two things in common, the ability to work hard and having amazing customer service skills. Stories that have been shared over the past eleven years of knowing them have revealed to me that small business ownership is not easy, yet there are many pros to being the man or woman in charge. My wife's aunt owns another large salon, meanwhile her uncle owns a big real estate firm. One of her cousins is also married to a family that has a huge construction company. Small businesses seem to "run in the family." None of these people went to college, but stirred up the entrepreneurial spirit that has afforded them all a livelihood in careers that have been enjoyable, meaningful, and have paid the bills.

Small Business Pros

One of the major benefits and arguably the most beneficial pro for owning a small business is indeed being the boss. There is nothing quite like working for yourself and calling all the shots. Having seen this with those in my wife's family over the years, as well as working alongside my two close friends who own the small business I now work for, NOVUS Clothing Company, it is clear that this is a key benefit. Being able to make the decisions from the small details of the day to the most important one's regarding personnel, finances, the mission and vision of the company, as well as any and all changes over the years is huge. The harder you work, the more profit you can make for the company, which essentially means more money in your pocket. This is a second benefit of owning and operating a small business. There really is no ceiling when it comes to earning potential and where you can take your business in this global economy we are part of in the 21st Century. This sense of limitless potential is often what attracts people from the start and motivates them. In addition, having complete autonomy to do something you truly believe in and enjoy is a great perk of a small business. Being able to set the work schedule, hire who you want on your team, oversee all operations, and have a direct hand in every aspect is important to many small business owners. As a result of the size staying small in nature, there is more of a family feel and intimacy that can benefit the business. The workers often have more of a stake in the business, a voice that can be heard since there are less employees, and ability to offer important advice that can be utilized. Along with the independence, control, prestige, equity, and networking opportunities that can come a small business owner's way includes financial gain.

Financial gain and benefit of a small business can be quite profitable. To add onto the flexibility and pursuing your passion, small businesses lead one to build a wealth making machine when an idea takes off, there is response to a necessary service, or one comes up with some kind of economic platform that helps society grow. Some other benefits of small businesses include and are not limited to the following:

- Preventative health and wellness programs.
- Flexible work schedules.
- Professional, career and educational support.
- Financial rewards or bonuses.
- Child care or eldercare support.
- Social activities.

Although not all of these are 100% financially driven, they all play into why people tend to want to operate small businesses. There are tax benefits also, which is important to outline. The majority of these benefits come from being able to make write offs. Small business ownership helps one reduce their overall tax liability by being able to write off the cost of the mortgage interest for their building or property each year as well as many other components. Business owners can utilize other tax breaks, such as the depreciated value of an automobile, equipment that is used for the job or business, areas of employee pay, retirement contributions, and facets as specific as car mileage. Below are some of the other tax benefits and write off opportunities for small business owners:

- Home Office
- Bonus Depreciation
- Professional Services
- Salaries and Wages
- Work Opportunity Tax Credit
- Office Supplies and Expenses
- Client and Employee Entertainment

As Farrah Gray put it, "Build your own dreams, or someone else will hire you to build theirs." There are several reasons why small businesses are often more likely to deliver and be successful and that is by offering better customer service than a large company and having increased customer knowledge. Also, because a smaller company is closer to its customers, it requires fewer resources to learn what people in their market desire. This allows them to focus more time and attention on meeting their customers expectations or exceeding them. Doing so most often results in a profitable business. Having worked at NOVUS Clothing Company, a small business which excels in custom sports apparel, it has been clear why small businesses are great. You cannot beat it when things are going well and the camaraderie can be next level.

The Cons of Small Businesses

Along with the good and the benefits of owning and operating a small business, inevitably come the cons. Like most things, it is important to examine both sides fully in order to make an informed decision. Being part of a small business, as well as hearing all of the stories, there are some key takeaways that must be shared for why small businesses are not always all that and a bag of chips per say. One thing I must put out there from the onset is that the majority of business owners, whether they are family or not, are certainly not going to discuss failures as much as their success. No one likes to air their dirty laundry or speak of all of the times when they were in a hole, the idea flopped, couldn't make payroll, or were on the brink of bankruptcy. And yet, all of these are risks that go into owning a small business. Having complete control and independence as good as it may seem, comes at a cost as well. This often means that you cannot ever escape your business because you are the one who is in charge. I have seen this working with a small business that the calls don't stop and the late night emails and texts seem to never go away. There is no such thing as leaving it at the office. That doesn't exist, as the office is always with you. Some people like this and are empowered by such a situation, while others hate it and claim it is ruining their life and relationships. In addition, the extra stress that comes barreling down on you each month to make the schedules, assign tasks and jobs to your employees, make all of the difficult decisions in terms of hires and firings, ensuring there is enough money to make payroll, and still keeping your own life outside of the business afloat can be brutal.

If you are not a person who likes stepping into a pressure cooker or having to bear the brunt of everything, maybe you ought to think twice. Keep in mind, owning a small business is not for the faint of heart. Let's examine the cons specifically when it comes to finances. Your business can clearly be a money pit and lead to a downfall in terms of bleeding your bank accounts. Pride often gets the most of small business owners who continue to fall and run in the red, as profits have gone by the wayside and they are incurring more and more debt. As a result of the ego getting in the way, people often hold onto their failing business for far too long. Instead of cutting losses and then still having to pay back all of that debt, they keep trying and go more into the red. Meanwhile, the business has flopped a while ago and is soon to close. This is a nightmare of a situation to say the least. When you own it, you own all of it and have to be the one who faces these financial issues head on. Everyone else has the ability to walk away and move on. For you, the small business owner, there is no getting around it, no bail out, and no hiding. The problem with finances comes and it is solely up to you to deal with it. That is intense. Along with significant financial risk come a number of other factors that make small business ownership a sizable challenge. The include and are not limited to:

- Covering Health Care for oneself and employees
- Government Regulations
- Federal Income Taxes and State Taxes
- Economic Swings
- Tax Compliance
- Cash Flow
- A Non Diversified Client Bases
- Bonus Depreciation

My hope is that before one even starts to compile a strategic plan to open a small business, they think about what each of the above can mean in the short term and over the long run. Other drawbacks or cons can include the fact that small businesses have less brand recognition, can experience higher costs, and operate on smaller budgets. This often poses a challenge when starting up because people do not know who you are or how reputable your service or product is. It can take a ton of time to build up a clientele base, grow to the point of recognition from competitors, and make a splash in saturated markets.

A good friend of mine and successful businessman was kind enough to contribute some great tips for people who desire to develop their own small business. Greg Aidala, an award winning actor and esteemed comedian, knows a ton about show business and taking center stage. For years Greg has grown his business and brand. He is often seen nowadays on tour as part of the Brew Haha Comedy Showcase bringing joy to people through his talent and comic relief. This is what Greg espouses in his talks and the strategic game plan he outlines for people who desire to win from the onset of their business journey:

1) Have a sound financial plan. Seeking out advisors and mentors that are trustworthy and of course well-versed is crucial.

2) Do your research. Researching other businesses related to the one you want to start is key. See what has worked for those companies, and use that information to implement your ideas.

3) Know that starting a business comes with great sacrifice & dedication.
You will need to have stellar organizational skills, be a proponent of time management, and never stop learning.

As you can see, owning a small business is quite the challenge. There are both advantages and disadvantages with regard to small business ownership. If you decide to start your own business, I highly suggest doing so after you are personally debt free and have a paid for home or a very low cost residence. Being smart with your money, whether it is completely for you and your family or to be utilized to run and own a business is key. Risk must be factored in and a budget must be adhered to. Having a well written game plan and strategy, as well as knowing what each facet will cost may help, but there are no guarantees. You don't know unless you try. This area of the financial realm is certainly not for everyone. I will leave you with a quote from Lindsay Manseau, an award winning freelance photographer who has taken the plunge to run her small business with great success as she shares, "Starting your own business is like riding a roller coaster. There are highs and lows and every turn you take is another twist. The lows are really low, but the highs can be really high. You have to be strong, keep your stomach tight, and ride along with the roller coaster that you started."

CHALLENGE #18: If you desire to begin a business, become informed, heed advice, and start small.

Before you jump right in and start your very own small business making it your entire livelihood, I challenge you to begin really small. Start with an area you are very knowledgeable about and understand thoroughly. Speak to others in that field of business, especially in the specific sector and get incite into what made them successful. Acquire as much information as possible from business owners that you can trust to gain knowledge about what they would have done differently. Make sure to have a number of trusted peers review your business plan as well. Then, starting very small, give it a shot. You never know until you try. Hopefully you don't have to lay out too much capital or risk a sizable amount of cash in order to see if this will be something you enjoy. The future will be a tell all of if your business will benefit your wealth building portfolio.

"Financial fitness is not a pipe dream or a state of mind. It's a reality if you are willing to pursue it and embrace it."

– Will Robinson

CHAPTER 19:
Creating Your Financial Blueprint

Construction is a beautiful thing. It involves a ton of planning, execution, effort, and progress management. Throughout the process one can track the headway that is being made and the results are tangible. Having the opportunity to build is something unique, takes great resources, and will leave a lasting mark for all to see. A master carpenter or foreman is intentional about everything they do on the job. He or she has been well educated, sharpened their skill set, and has a well equipped tool belt to draw upon in order to create a masterpiece. Little by little, day by day, the building takes form. Over the course of time the end product will be complete and the crew chief will be able to smile knowing that everything that had to come together did in order to complete the build. Chances are that the edifice that was constructed will remain there for a long time and for many years it will be enjoyed.

You are the architect of your financial freedom and future. The very blueprints that are to be written and used as the game plan to allow you to execute the master build with your money must be written. This blueprint will serve as the skeleton, game plan, and instruction manual to fabricate a superstructure over the years that lie ahead. Perhaps you are thinking, well this is quite a daunting task. I have so many changes that need to be made to my plan. Others could have thoughts that are rolling around in their mind such as, I had no plan at all, but it is time that I got started. Wherever you are in your financial journey, creating a specific and systematic blueprint that covers the bases of the areas we have discussed will be crucial for you to have a successful build. Soon it will be time to break ground if you haven't done so already. Without a plan, you are basically shooting darts in the dark and merely hoping to get lucky. That approach will allow one to hit every once in a while. We are looking for far greater results. No master builder sets a single nail without first developing an in depth and detailed approach beforehand. Lay it all out on paper and if you have a spouse or significant other, ensure that you discuss this thoroughly as a team.

The first step for creating your financial blueprint is to have what we call the dream meeting. I suggest that you take some time to ponder what your short term, mid term, and long term goals are. What are your aspirations for life? How can your finances and taking complete ownership over your money allow you to reach these goals? Brainstorm them, write them down, and make sure that they are what we call *SMART* goals (Specific, Measurable, Attainable, Relevant, and Time Oriented). Hold your dream meeting where you talk about each of these goals in detail. Discuss the importance of them or if you are single, think about each. Concentrate on three things: 1) What do you want? 2) How will you get there 3) Why is it important to you? The most important component of the dream meeting is to devote enough time to go over the two biggest questions outlined above, namely WHY? and HOW? In life, whether it be with finances or basically anything that is important to us, when our WHY is big enough, we will be willing to do whatever it takes to achieve it. You must have reasons for creating this game plan. Your specific financial blueprint must have goals tied to it and a reason otherwise there is no point. Next, think about and discuss how you will achieve those goals. Use the SMART goal formula when creating or constructing an updated budget. One might create a goal that looks similar to this example below:

S- I will compute and calculate all of my bills, expenses, debts, and income
M- by using the 3 month expenditure assessment tool to track all money earned & spent.
A- This will be completed daily and reported to my accountability partner weekly
R- because it will help me take ownership and reach my first goal of saving $1,000
T- within a three month period to help build my new budget & achieve baby step 1.

In the above SMART goal we targeted and ran through each criteria through a systematic and specific approach. As the goal is accomplished, no matter how small or large it might be, you should check it off and recognize your achievement. This is like completing phase one of your build as a construction foreman. It is important to recognize the efforts that were made by one's team and that is no doubt you will enjoy seeing progress. When progress occurs it helps to keep us motivated and hungry. We will then work hard to achieve phase two and so on. The blueprint we write and create can always be tweaked as we go along, as it is not set in stone. However, like any wise builder, a wise investor uses the knowledge they have acquired to build the very best structure. The goal is to create a product that will last for a long time, be extremely functional, and is cost efficient.

The second step is the continual monitoring of how your plan is working. This is done by doing monthly budget balances and check ins with your accountability partner. Step two will keep you moving forward toward your goals, as well as staying on track without veering way off course. Challenge yourself and your accountability partner to have an even better month ahead. Create a small goal for the specific month you are entering. If you are paying down debt, set a target amount you desire to annihilate and then go after it with all your effort. Small goals will add up toward helping you reach your larger and more long term goals through this systematic approach.

The third step is to increase your income level. Throughout the book we have discussed at length the numerous ways one can utilize various forms of income streams to power-up their pockets. Creating the so-called green machine for yourself is possible, but it takes changes and more focus. Be intentional about picking up extra shifts at work, a second part time job, and my favorite one, installing passive income streams into your repertoire. Allow the money you make go to work for you. Doing this will help you to carry out that financial blueprint and most likely add some beautiful finishes to your master build along the way. The more money that you have coming in, the more room for investments, choices to get behind the wheel of different financial vehicles, and increased cash flow that will help to accelerate the process. Jim Rohn, who amassed a net worth of over $500 million as a successful entrepreneur, businessman, and renowned author put it into perspective nicely when he stated, "I remember saying to my mentor, 'If I had more money, I would have a better plan.' He quickly responded, 'I would suggest that if you had a better plan, you would have more money.' You see, it's not the amount that counts; it's the plan that counts." Create that blueprint and stick to the plan!

Finally, there is great value in seeing your financial blueprint on a regular basis. Put your written down goals and dreams on sticky notes, tape them to your bathroom mirror or tack them up on some other visual display. Always keep those in the forefront of your mind. Do not forget about the WHY! You are carrying out a game plan and doing something that is not easy, yet will literally pay you great dividends both now in the present and for the rest of your life. If you need some support or a kick in the butt for motivation, simply pick up the phone and talk to your accountability partner. If you are searching for some answers, re-read a section of this book or acquire another text that will educate you. Remember, knowledge is power. Your money can build something pretty amazing and provide the life that you always wanted. There is no substitute for your consistent efforts, planning, discipline, and desire.

CHALLENGE #19: Begin Building Your Financial Blueprint.

Sit down this week and start out with your why. Think about all of your dreams for your life. Jot them down and use those to conduct a dream meeting. Start writing down specific short term, mid, and long term financial goals for your future. Based on these goals, be honest with yourself and/or your spouse. Think about what necessary adjustments you must make to develop a winning financial blueprint. Kick those bad habits to the curb. After you have everything out, post your blueprint somewhere so you can visualize it regularly. Ensure it stays at the forefront of your mind. Take the first step forward and begin to carry out your new financial plan. Little by little you will build your future life and get closer to financial freedom.

"If you want to be financially free you need to become a different person than you are today and let go of whatever has held you back in the past."

-Robert Kiyosaki

CHAPTER 20: Closing Thoughts

Money matters and it makes sense to use the dollars we work so hard for to better our lives. Going green in the 21st Century when it comes to our finances is all about having the ability to provide ourselves and those we love with a choice filled life. Time is money and in the same wavelength, money is time. You and I might be common people, but we have the opportunity to build an uncommon future. Your willingness to commit and the effort that you put into this will yield tremendous results. However, it all comes down to one's discipline and drive. What do you want your story to be? You are the author of your life and it just so happens that money provides the gateway to doing some incredible things. The experiences, memories, and opportunities that you have are very much aligned to how you utilize your wallet on a daily basis. It comes down to dollars and sense.

Quality of life is something that all people should have. I desire that each person is able to feel safe, be comfortable in their home, be well fed, and have the material goods necessary to be more than okay. Enjoying the things we love most whether that be spending time with our family or friends, engaging in a fun activity, or taking part in a hobby that makes one happy is what life can provide. The currency that runs through our society and pulls us like a river in various directions can be quite challenging. Money is so simple, yet so hard to manage. It is so important and we need it, yet at times it can become all consuming and take us away from what matters most.

My hope is that you have gained significant knowledge by reading this book and that your financial tool belt is now more well equipped. It was my purpose and goal to lay out a way for you to make choices to reach financial freedom and have renewed peace in your life. Money can be our greatest cause of stress and the thing that becomes our arch enemy. Meanwhile, there are ways for us to flip that script and use the everyday dollar to empower us and create a life where we thrive. No one and nobody can stop you. Like Dr. Seuss says in his book *Oh The Places You Will Go,* "You have brains in your head and feet in your shoes, you can steer yourself in any way you choose." So what will your choice be? How will you be different today than you were yesterday? How will you decide to improve your life and provide a better path for your kids and grandchildren? When will you look yourself in the mirror and come to terms with the debt you are in? What will you change in order to capitalize on making money through sound investments and saving more than you are spending? When are you going to take the first step toward financial freedom?

Today is your day. It is time for you to implement that financial blueprint. You have what it takes to be uncommon and live differently. Yeah, there will be a lot of temptation along your journey to go back to old ways. Many people will try to pull you away from the new path you have laid out. It will be hard at times and discipline won't feel good. You may even want to quit and might find yourself with the towel in your hand ready to toss it in once and for all. Or just maybe you will stay persistent, determined, hard working, driven, and motivated. Maybe this time around you will have your eyes and mindset fixated on winning. Maybe this will be the day, month, and year that you flip your financial future upside down and start creating a better life that is yours for the taking. Remember, slow and steady wins the race and financial independence can be achieved. It is time for you to take complete ownership over your life and that begins by owning your finances. Tell your money where to go and make it become your greatest asset. Build an empire and flood your future with dreams that you will choose to come true. As the great Michael Jordan said so powerfully, "Some people want it to happen, some wish it would happen, and others make it happen." This is your life. It is your golden nest egg we are talking about. We all have to start somewhere. Take those baby steps and make it happen. Follow the plan and watch your blueprint build a tremendous future. I cannot guarantee the final dollar amount that will be in your portfolio or accurately predict how wealthy you will be if you do X, Y, or Z. What I can guarantee is that by reaching your goals, living out your dreams, and achieving financial independence, you will absolutely have increased peace and enjoy life more. You will undoubtedly change the financial game you are playing and be able to afford things you never could before. And you will be able to in many ways take back time, while enjoying those precious moments a little bit more with those you care about most. Fire up that green machine! It is time for us to make some money!

Challenge #20: Begin Your Journey

The final challenge of the book is for you to take that first step or begin the path of renewal. This is the hardest, but the most critical one to take. Setting the ball into motion and actually doing it is not easy. I hope that you feel inspired and well equipped to take that initial step toward a better and brighter future. For some of you this is the starting block, you are ready to run the race. For others, it is time to get back on the horse and ride better than ever until you reach the winner's circle. Wherever you are on the journey, keep progressing. It will be well worth it!

Acknowledgments:

It has long been a goal of mine to write a book on the topic of finances. Since I was a young kid I have always had an interest and desire to make money. Having the opportunity to share knowledge about finances and support to people has been fun. My main drive with this text was to provide my audience with the resources, tools, and strategies that can help them win with their money. As an educator, I take great pride in passing along information that will better the lives of others. I hope that you will do the same and share your knowledge. This book would not have been possible without the support of so many tremendous individuals. I want to thank my wife for always supporting my endeavors and being the best teammate possible. Her encouragement along the way, willingness to stick to our financial blueprint, and work hard to achieve the goals we have has been exceptional.

This book was a long time in the making. I believe that it began decades ago as a child growing up. I want to thank my parents for teaching me the value of money and showing me how to save. The discipline I witnessed and how you were financially responsible has stuck with me. You laid a rock solid foundation many years ago that has certainly provided the groundwork which I have continued to build upon as an adult. In addition, I have to give great credit to some extraordinary financial minds and people that have been mentors to me over the years. I appreciate and am grateful for the likes of Dave Ramsey, Chris Hogan, Benjamin Graham, Warren Buffet, and the FIRE Community. The books, radio shows, podcasts, and motivational talks that I have listened to have really inspired me to become a winner with my finances.

Lastly, I want to thank each of you for taking the time and spending the money to invest in my book. I applaud you for doing so. This was a choice you made and I hope you feel it was worth every minute and every penny. Thank you for going on this journey with me and for taking each challenge seriously. It is now my hope that you share this resource with others and apply the knowledge you gained to achieve your dreams!

References

Clason, George S. *The Richest Man in Babylon.* 1926.

Graham, Benjamin. *The Intelligent Investor: The Definitive Book on Value Investing.* HarperCollins Publishers: New York, New York. 2020.

Hogan, Chris. *Everyday Millionaire.* Ramsey Press: Mahwah, New Jersey. 2019.

Hogan, Chris. *Retire Inspired.* Ramsey Press: Mahwah, New Jersey. 2016.

Memula, Chris, Barrett, Brade, Mendonsa, Jonathan. *Choose FI: Your Blueprint to Financial Independence.* BiggerPockets Publishing LLC: Denver, Colorado. 2019.

Ramsey, Dave. *The Total Money Makeover.* Thomas Nelson: Nashville, Tennessee 2003.

Ramsey, Dave. *Financial Peace University.* 1994. Ramsey Solutions.

Ramsey, Dave. *Completed Guide to Money.* Ramsey Press: Mahwah, New Jersey. 2011.

Rieckens, Scott. *Playing With Fire: Financial Independence Retire Early.* New World Library: Novato, California. 2019.

Turner, Brandon. *The Book on Rental Property Investing: How to Create Wealth and Passive Income Through Intelligent Buy & Hold Real Estate Investing.* Bigger Pockets Publishing LLC. 2015

APPENDIX

In this section of the text, you will find an arrangement of materials, knowledge, website links and insight from experts in the financial field. Along with my own thoughts and analysis come great pieces of advice from the likes of Dave Ramsey, Chris Hogan, and others. This blend of resources, anecdotal summations, and conclusions should aid your journey of achieving financial freedom. My main goal has always been and will continue to be helping you get your peace back by taking complete ownership of your money!

The Baby Step Bible

The following compilation of notes & resources comes from the influential teachings and financial ways of world renowned guru, Dave Ramsey.

Baby Step 1 – SAVE 1,000 to start an Emergency Fund. In this first step, your goal is to save $1,000 as fast as you can. And not just "fast." We're talking as fast as you can! Your emergency fund will cover those unexpected life events you can't plan for. Without an emergency fund, most people feel like they have to go into debt to cover surprise expenses like a busted pipe or medical bills. But not you! You're not doing debt anymore.

Keep your emergency fund in a separate checking account so you won't spend it accidentally (or on purpose) on things that aren't actually emergencies. You don't want to dig a deeper hole while you're trying to work your way out of debt! So, how do you start the process of saving up for your emergency fund? Step one of step one is to make a budget.

•

Baby Step 2 – Pay off all debt using the Debt Snowball (including college loans, cars, credit cards, etc...All things outside of your Mortgage) Now it's time to pay off all that nasty debt you're ready to get rid of. Start by listing all of your debts you owe on outside of your mortgage. The cars. The student loans. The credit cards. The store cards. The gas cards. Yikes, that's a lot—but don't stop now! Put them in order by balance from smallest to largest. Don't worry about interest rates unless two debts have similar balances —then you'll list the debt with a higher interest rate first. This is called the debt snowball method, and you'll use it to knock out your debts one by one.

Now it's time to attack the first balance on your list. Pay as much as you can each month while making the minimum payments on your other debts. We mean go after it! Sell everything you can. Get a second job. Sell so much the kids think they're next! You want to get rid of that payment quickly. When you've paid it off, add those payments to the monthly payment on your next debt and start attacking it.

It's hard work, but this is what winning looks like! The small wins you make at the beginning will keep you motivated to dump all your debt. And before you know it, you're debt free! Millions of people have used the proven program, Financial Peace University, to learn how to never worry about money again.

Baby Step 3 – SAVE 3 to 6 months of expenses in savings (Emergency fund) You've paid off your debt! Way to go! But don't slow down now. It's time to take that money you were throwing at your debt and build your full emergency fund to cover 3–6 months of your expenses. We know that sounds like a lot of money, but it should be! You want this to protect you against life's bigger surprises like the loss of a job or your car breaking down. With that much cash saved up, you won't have to slip back into debt to cover these emergencies.

Put this savings in your emergency savings or money market account so you won't be tempted to touch it. Trust us, you'd be tempted! (We're looking at you, yearly trip to that beachfront condo right next to that little seafood buffet place with the crab wontons.)

Baby Step 4 – Invest 15% of household income into Roth IRAs and pre-tax retirement. In this step, it's time to get serious about retirement—no matter your age. This is when you take 15% of your gross household income and start investing it into your retirement.

Start by investing enough in your company 401(k) plan to receive the full employer match. Hey, that's free money! Then invest the rest into Roth IRAs—one for you and one for your spouse (if you're married). If your company doesn't offer a retirement plan or match your contributions, then go straight to the Roth IRA. We get it. Investing is a boring subject. But when you see your money growing like beautiful weeds, it won't seem so boring!

If you're not too sure about what you're doing, an investing professional can help you find the right funds and make sure you're on the right track.

Baby Step 5 – College funding for children By this step, you've paid off all debts but the house and started saving for retirement. Now it's time to save for your children's college expenses. That is if they make it through Algebra II and Chemistry unscathed. Saving will put you ahead of the game when your teens graduate from high school. Trust us on this one. It happens fast! If your kids are already in high school, it's not too late! You'll just need to set aside your money a little faster.

Two smart ways to save for your children's college when they're still little are 529 college savings plans or ESAs (Education Savings Accounts). These options will save you a bundle in taxes and are specifically designed for college expenses.

But before you choose either option, do your homework! Depending on your income and what state you live in, a 529 might be better than an ESA. And just like with mutual funds for retirement, an investing professional can help you figure this out.

Baby Step 6 – Pay off home early Now it's time to bring it all home. Baby Step 6 is the big dog! There's only one more thing standing in the way of complete freedom from debt—and that's your mortgage. Can you imagine your life with no house payment?

Any extra money you can put toward your mortgage could save you tens (or even hundreds) of thousands in interest. If you currently have an adjustable-rate, interest-only or even 30-year mortgage, consider refinancing to a 15-year, fixed-rate mortgage. You'll be amazed at how much you can save in the long run!

Baby Step 7 – Build wealth and give! You know what people with no debt can do? Anything they want! Baby Step 7 is the last and can be the most fun step.

Now you can live and give like no one else! This is where you keep building wealth and become insanely generous. Imagine what it would feel like to be able to leave an inheritance for your kids and their kids. That's all possible now because you had discipline for a few years. Now that's what we call leaving a legacy!

Your perseverance and good habits are what will get you there. Keep setting goals and budgeting every month. Max out your 401(k) and Roth IRAs so you can continue to live and give like no one else—even in retirement.

When you reach your financial goals, help someone else get started on their own journey. One great way to do that is with our most popular bundle, The Starter Special.

FIVE Things that will Make You Wealthy

1) Have a written game plan (Budget) "For which one of you, when he wants to build a tower, does not first sit down and calculate the cost to see if he has enough to complete it" Luke 14:28 -NO ONE ACCIDENTALLY WINS AT ANYTHING

2) GET OUT OF DEBT -Greatest wealth building tool is your income. With no payments you have money $.

3) Live on less than you make. "In the house of the wise are stores of choice food and oil, but a foolish man devours all he has." (Proverbs 21:20) If you spend everything you make, you are a fool. -You only get stagnant wages if you stay stagnant. Stagnant pond water grows scum on top. Have the attitude that says, "I am going to control the controllable."

4) Save some money $ -Rich people get rich by saving money. 100% of people who build wealth save money. You need investments like mutual funds, stocks, and real estate to win.

5) Be outrageously & randomly generous. Broke people can't do that.

Debt Snowball Summary: How to Pay Off Debt

What could you do if you didn't have a single debt payment in the world? That's right—no student loans, car payments or credit card bills! For some of you, that would free up an extra $300, $500, or maybe even $800 a month. Ah, that's the debt free life. The quickest way to make your debt-free dream a reality is to use the debt snowball method.

What Is the Debt Snowball Method? The debt snowball method is a debt reduction strategy in which you pay off bills in order of smallest to largest, regardless of interest rate. But it's more than a method for paying off bills. The debt snowball is designed to help you change how you behave with money so you never go into debt again. It forces you to stay intentional about paying one bill at a time until you're debt-free. And it gives you power over your debt. When you pay off that first bill and move on to the next, you'll see that debt is not the boss of your money. You are.

This is how the debt snowball method works:

Step 1: List your debts from smallest to largest.

Step 2: Make minimum payments on all debts except the smallest—throwing as much money as you can at that one. Once that debt is gone, take its payment and apply it to the next smallest debt while continuing to make minimum payments on the rest.

Step 3: Repeat this method as you plow your way through debt. The more you pay off, the more your freed-up money grows—like a snowball rolling downhill. If you begin with the biggest debt, you won't see traction for a long time. You might think you're not making fast enough progress and then lose steam and quit before you even get close to finishing. It's important to pay your debts in a way that keeps you motivated until you've wiped them out. Getting quick wins in the beginning will light a fire under you to pay off your remaining debts! Listen—knock out that smallest debt first, and you will find the motivation to go the distance. Great personal finances don't happen by chance. They happen by choice.

What Should I Include in my Debt Snowball? Now you're thinking like a money pro. Your debt snowball should include all non- mortgage debt—debt being defined as anything you owe to anyone else. (Though your mortgage is technically debt, we don't include it in the debt snowball.)

Examples of non-mortgage debt:

Payday loans, student loans, medical bills, car notes, credit card balances, home equity loans, personal loans. And by the way, there's no such thing as great debt. Take student loans, for example. Many consider student loans worthwhile debt, but the truth is, they hurt your finances in the long run. Think about it. Student loan repayment can seriously delay a person's ability to buy a home, save money, and invest for the future. The bottom line is that no debt is good debt.

Listen Now: What's the Reason for the Debt Snowball?

When am I ready to start the Debt Snowball? You're ready to begin your debt snowball once you've saved your $1,000 starter emergency fund. That's what we call Baby Step #1. An emergency fund covers those life events you can't plan for. Think busted hot water heater, dental emergency or flat tire. You get the drift. An emergency fund protects you from having to go further into debt to pay for an unexpected expense. So with that said, you'll start your debt snowball on Baby Step #2. That means you're current on all your bills and have completed Baby Step #1.

RETIREMENT BASICS & Resources
(Chris Hogan)

https://www.chrishogan360.com/

This site is awesome to gain more knowledge on retirement and how much you will need based on the life you want to have during retirement. It goes hand in hand with RETIRE INSPIRED (book).

https://www.chrishogan360.com/category/investing-basics

Retirement savings done now and budgeted beginning now (every month) will be the best habit you can get into and it will PAYOFF, literally in hundreds of thousands and even millions later on. Those who do it now learn that it is a part of the regular monthly budget and it's no burden. Those who don't lose out on compound interest and they don't want to do so much later on...resulting in problems down the road. This article is very short but explains it all and shows a graphic:

RIQ: Retirement calculator for how much you will need to retire by the desired age and how much you will have to put away/save per month to hit your goal:

HOGAN'S RETIREMENT BASICS:
A. Retirement is not an age thing it is about having the financial resources to live out your dream.

B. Dream so you have a goal.

C. *Most importantly have a plan and stick to the plan so you can reach the dream. Be intentional and take action!

D. Retirement is not an old person thing, but a smart person thing and a focused person thing that takes sacrifice. (LIVE LIKE NO ONE ELSE SO YOU CAN LIVE & GIVE LIKE NO ONE ELSE)

The 4 Fundamentals of an Inspired Retirement:

1) Dreaming -Keep your eyes on the prize of your "want tos" so the turn into get tos 2) Planning -Budget & strategic plan over the long haul to build your retirement. 15% in growth stock mutual funds. 3) Execution -Follow through with the plan. Avoid debt & stupid financial decisions- stay the course. 4) Commitment -Sacrifices are going to be made to reach the goal. Continue to do what it takes while maintaining relationships. 5) Vigilance -Protect your retirement dream and legacy. Don't let STUPID lurk in. Don't compare yourself to others...run your own race. *100% of the stock market's 15 year periods have gained money since inception. That's a sound investment.

Compound interest: When you invest and earn interest at a percentage you then earn interest on the interest as it compounds...$1,000 invested at 10%= $1,100 after year 1...$1,100 invested at 10%= $1,210 after 5 years $1,610...after 40 years your $1,000 investment without adding a $1 has turned into $45,000 (by sitting for 40 years at 10%) WOW! **$50,000 invested at 8% over 10 years--> $107,946, after 30 years-->$503,132, after 40 years $1,086,226 * "Compound interest is the 8th wonder of the world." -Albert Einstein *Compound interest is like Chinese bamboo trees...The tree takes 5 years after being planted to break the surface of the ground and then it grows exponentially and you can literally see it grow! By investing in one's Roth IRA at $5,500 invested per year over 30 years growing tax free (@10%) you will sit at $1,091,160... For only $458/month Compound interest calculator: **http:// www.moneychimp.com/calculator/ compound_interest_calculator.htm**

DCA (Dollar Cost Averaging) -When you invest an allotted amount every month over time spread out to get the best bang for your buck and most shares while the market fluctuates. (ex could invest $4,000 all at once and get 40 shares at $100/share...or use DCA and over a year/12 month span it could be as much as 55 shares because sometimes those shares will be lower than the $100 rate. --> With employee Match for retirement or putting in a monthly contribution this creates a DCA for you already.

4 Types of Asset Classes to Invest In

1) CASH-- Savings, checking, money market, CDs (certificate of deposit) all good for safe short term savings. Have to be careful because inflation is

2.5-3%/yr and banks offer virtually no interest.

2) BOND ASSETS (Loaning money for a return & interest...similar to being a personal bank) --> Bonds are loan agreements between a borrower and investor...The borrower pays the investor a set % of interest over a specific amount of time. A)Treasury bond- backed by US gov't/treasury -6% return over / years (Pay fed tax on interest earned) B) Municipal bond- issued by state and local governments as tax shelters...over 30-40 years mature and receive interest earned usually federal tax free & sometimes state Tax free C) Corporate Bonds-- offered by companies..loan money to them at a fixed % interest and they pay back over set amount of time...risky but higher yield. -When bond reaches maturity date the borrower pays back the original amount. (The interest paid per year is called the "coupon" & it's paid every year until the bond reaches maturity)

3) STOCK ASSETS -Owning little pieces of a company *Buy low and sell high - You receive money when stock goes up in value and you get a dividend payout by the company for a "thanks" for continuing to support the company when they are doing well quarterly. It is more risky to invest in single stocks, while it is a safer bet to invest in mutual funds.

4)REAL ESTATE ASSETS - Investing in land or anything permanently fixed to it (house, apartment, building, etc) A)Residential-- investing in homes B) Commercial C) Industrial. Only invest in real estate when you have the cash on hand to purchase the property in full because you want to mitigate risk moving to retirement. Having a mortgage heightens risk. People have to have an emergency fund In place for the real estate and also factor in property taxes, homeowners insurance and interest.

*Mutual Funds- The best way to invest by mutually going in on investments with a number of companies. The name of a mutual fund is the type it is (I.e.: Bond Mutual Fund, International. Stock Mutual Fund, etc.)

4 MOST COMMON MUTUAL FUNDS IN 401Ks & Retirement Plans

1) Growth & Income (predictable, safer, more calm)

2) Growth (stable, mid line aggression/payout vs risk)

3) Aggressive Growth ("wild child funds" very risky and a wild card)

4) International (companies around the world)

Small Cap=Smaller capital companies with smaller Amounts of money - Companies below $2 Billion

Large Cap=Large Capital or very high amounts of money in that company/company's worth (Above $10Billion)

Mid Cap= Middle (Between $2- $10 Billion) Mutual funds invest in a number of different companies for example and your return is based on how the companies grow over time. Some go up and some down, but the overall mixed bag goes up over time.

SHIELDING INVESTMENT FROM TAXES

Tax Favored plans--> Tax deferred plans like 401K or 403B because money comes out before (pre-taxes) and this allows you to invest it and not pay taxes on it now so it doesn't count against you when you file your taxes at end of year...However you must pay taxes on the money when taking it out later on. A Roth IRA & Roth 401K are tax free plans because you find them with after tax dollars and they grow tax free.

Qualified Plan= A retirement plan that is established by an employer for all employees

1) Defined Benefit plan (pension)= guaranteed payout

2) Defined contribution (employee match). Bylaws outline when the money can be touched without penalty.

Non-Qualified Plan- any tax deferred employer-sponsored plan that does not meet requirements set by the employee retirement income security act.

1) Deferred compensation plans

2) Executive bonus plans

3) Group Carve out plans

4) Split dollar insurance plans

Note: 401K and 403B are just the numbers on the tax forms for deferred taxation...mutual funds are what you invest in.

-If your company offers a ROTH 401K, take that option because you will pay tax on your contributions and it will grow tax free. If there is an employer match then that means the matching contribution will be in a separate account growing and be taxed upon taking the money out.

IRA (Individual Retirement Arrangement) -Tax deferred treatment--> Can have mutual funds, annuities, and even real estate in your IRA)

When changing jobs do a direct rollover into an IRA and a direct transfer right into the new IRA. NEVER take the money out/home or have it go to You or you will pay lots of taxes and fees.

BEST RETIREMENT PLAN -After you are debt free contribute 15% of income into retirement -If employer offers match do the max match contribution and then put the rest in the Roth IRA. If you max out the Roth IRA and have money left over to hit the 15% mark then put the remainder in 401K with the company. After paying off your house, contribute more to retirement but realize you cannot touch money until 59 1/2 years old. -So if desired to retire early have money saved to live on for the years between retirement and 59 1/2 years old.

SOCIAL SECURITY (SS) -Icing on the cake during retirement. Full retirement age for 100% SS benefit is age 67. You can collect at age 62, but only get 70% of the benefit (bad plan).

-When collected at age 64=80% payout

-Age 65=85%

-Age 66=93%

-Age 67=100%

***If you wait to age 70=132% -->Note that once you collect that is the set percentage you get the rest of your life and it doesn't change. Sign up for Medicare at age 65 (totally separate from SS).

HSA- Health Savings accounts can save money in this plan if qualified (high deductible health insurance plans quality). You can invest the monies into various mutual funds and use it as another smaller retirement account. This is tax free and the use of money for any medical expense or money is available for withdrawal at age 59.5 (retirement) with a tax rate of 30% because they are pre taxed dollars.

What YOU SHOULD HAVE SAVED FOR RETIREMENT by AGE

**1x income by age 35, 3x income by age 45, 5x income by age 55, 7x income by age 62.

KISS Rule (Keep It Simple Stupid) Money is like manure, in one big pile it stinks, but spread out it grows things like crazy! Diversification lowers risk. Use mutual funds and spread it around by pooling funds of money to make something a mutual fund, a together investment. Look at the track records of the funds. Leave the money in for at least five years, so pick the best performing ones over a long haul.

HOME Ownership & Mortgages

Pay off your home early

-Hold budget accountable--> Look forward with your money. Become debt free and have an emergency fund in place before buying home. Home ownership is a forced savings plan->>wealth tool & inflation hedge. A house grows virtually tax free up to $500K when selling it.

1) Location is the key to a good home for resale.

2) Get a bargain- The home interior could be ugly, but you can fix that quickly. A home needs good curb appeal/view or water on the property. Always buy Title insurance.

Best way to buy a home: 100% down plan...focus 31% of homes don't have mortgage debt in US -Game plan 15 year fixed rate, at least 10% down and mortgage payment no more than 25% of income. A 15 year mortgage saves hundreds of thousands of $$dollars -Myth: Tax advantage on a mortgage--> There is no tax advantage that supersedes the amount you save by paying off the mortgage. -20% down then don't have to pay PMI. A conventional loan is the best one to get (Fannie Mae).

SELLING A HOME

Think like a retailer. Paint the picture the way it appears to sell the home. Take stuff off counters and box stuff in cabinets, put light bulbs in lots of lights on in the house! It makes it look big. Make sure the house smells good. What is the curb appeal? Put money to tune it up before it goes for sale. 90% of buyers see the picture from the curb. Do a CMA (comparative market analysis) so you know what your home is really worth versus the competition in your area that has sold.

20 TIPS from People Who are Winning with Money! (Dave Ramsey)

1. Keep your savings account at a different bank than your checking account. "That way you don't see your savings every time you log into your account. You won't be tempted to transfer it or use it. Out of sight, out of mind!" — Michelle M.

2. Use the budget to help you reach fun goals. A budget isn't something you have to do because you've been bad. It's something you do so you can be good. We're going to Disney and paying cash!" — Alex S.

3. Only buy what you need (and can afford). "Even though something is a good deal, it doesn't mean you should buy it." — Anne M.

4. What matters isn't how much you're allowed to borrow but how much you have in the bank. "Who cares about my FICO score? I don't." — Hyunmee P.

5. Don't let discouragement keep you from making a budget. "There's always hope when you have a plan." — Brandon C.

6. Go old school and balance your checking account. "This is essential! Balance your checking account so you know where you're at and then begin with a basic budget. **It's all about taking baby steps.**" — Kay N.

7. Give yourself some fun money so you'll stay on budget. "I was swiping my card for miscellaneous things. It turns out we were blowing the budget by $150 to $250 a month! I just needed to issue myself an envelope system for pocket money. Now I even have money left over at the end of the month!" — Rick M.

8. Say goodbye to *all* of your debt. "I grew up with the misconception that having car loans, a house loan and student loans was something everybody did when they got older. I don't consider myself debt-free simply because I don't have any credit card debt. My husband and I are working at paying off all of our debt!" — Amy M.

9. Be patient with purchases—and with yourself. "We learned to be patient while saving up cash to purchase a new appliance, go on vacation, or buy a car. We also spent over 20 years learning that debt was good, so it took some time to unlearn these things and replace them with new behaviors." — Katherine E.

10. Get on the same team with your spouse. "Sitting down together and going over the bills and budget has changed our marriage. **There are no more fights about money.** We budget together." — Trina G.

11. Set up a savings fund for irregular expenses. "My son had just started preschool when I took FPU, so we were in and out of the doctor's office every week. I now set aside a few dollars in my budget each week for copay and prescription costs. This is a godsend!" — Chloe C.

12. Don't believe everything society tells you about money. "Debt can steal your future. It's so important for kids to understand how to deal with money and debt—and what the consequences of their decisions will look like. **You can make better decisions when you know all the facts.**" — Susan K.

13. Be prepared for emergencies. "Having an emergency fund for a rainy day will prevent you from getting a credit card and falling into debt." — Hyunmee P.

14. Tell your money where to go. "We learned the importance of a budget and telling our money where to go. It works! We're now debt-free—that $89,000 owed is gone!" — Angelica A.

15. Put your long-term goals in the right order. "Retirement should come before saving for my child's college. I didn't really think that through before taking the FPU class." — Shawn H.

16. Use the envelope system. "Pull money out of your account and put it in envelopes. If it isn't in your envelope, you can't use your debit card. We found when we stopped using envelopes for a month we busted our budget. Back to envelopes it is!" — Jennifer B.

17. Talk with your lender to solve any problems while you're paying off debt. "Always work with your credit card companies. My bank overcharged me interest, and after we talked, they ended up sending me a check." — John S.

18. Embrace the power of cash. "I bought several cars with cash and saved on the purchase price. Also, letting go of cash in hand hurts. I've walked away from many purchases in order to keep the cash in my hand." — Desiree E.

19. Be generous. "The most important lesson I learned in FPU was to set myself up to be a blessing to others—whether it's by giving sound financial advice, helping people draft a monthly budget, or giving to someone anonymously." — Alexander H.

20. Make daily decisions with the end goal in mind. "The daily choices you make concerning your money dictate what options you will have. Sacrifice in the beginning reaps huge rewards in the end." — Shelle C.

Websites & Links:

Dave Ramsey Website: https://www.daveramsey.com/

There you can find links in the TOOLS for budgeting, paying off debt, saving for college, retirement, etc. **https://www.chrishogan360.com/**

Budgeting Tools: Every Dollar and the Every Dollar budgeting APP https://www.everydollar.com/ A site to help you personalize your families budget each month & track expenses/ savings. Zero Dollar Budget Sheet & expenditure inventory included.

The Dave Ramsey Show (Youtube Channel) https://www.youtube.com/user/DaveRamseyShow

Compound interest calculator: http://www.moneychimp.com/calculator/compound_interest_calculator.htm

retirement calculator http://www.moneychimp.com/calculator/retirement_calculator.htm

mortgage calculator http://www.moneychimp.com/calculator/retirement_calculator.htm

Other Great Financial Books:

The Infographic Guide to Personal Finance (Michele Cogan-CPA & Elisabeth Lariviere)

Rich Dad, Poor Dad (Richard Kiyosaki)

The Millionaire Next Door (Thomas J. Stanley)

The Simple Path to Wealth (JL Collins)

Broke Millennial (Erin Lowry)

Biblical Scripture & Money

"Lazy hands make for poverty, but diligent hands bring wealth." (Proverbs 10:4)

"The borrower is slave to the lender." (Proverbs 22:7)

"Honor the LORD with your wealth and with the first fruits of all your produce." (Proverbs 3:9)

"In the house of the wise are stores of choice food and oil." (Proverbs 21:20)

"For which one of you, when he wants to build a tower, does not first sit down and calculate the cost to see if he has enough to complete it?" (Luke 14:28)

"For the love of money is the root of all evil: which while some coveted after, they have erred from the faith, and pierced themselves through with many sorrows." (1 Timothy 6:10)

"God blesses the cheerful giver." (2 Corinthians 9:7)

Jesus Parable of the Talents: (Matthew 25:14-30)

"For to everyone who has will more be given, and he will have an abundance. But from the one who has not, even what he has will be taken away." (Matthew 25:29)

"For where your treasure is, there also will your heart be." (Matthew 6:21)

"Whoever loves money never has enough; whoever loves wealth is never satisfied with their income. This too is meaningless." (Ecclesiastes 5:10)

"Dishonest money dwindles away, but whoever gathers money little by little makes it grow." (Proverbs 13:11)

"Keep your lives free from the love of money and be content with what you have, because God has said, "Never will I leave you; never will I forsake." (Hebrews 13:5)

Jesus answered, "If you want to be perfect, go, sell your possessions and give to the poor, and you will have treasure in heaven. Then come, follow." (Matthew 19:21)

"No one can serve two masters. Either you will hate the one and love the other, or you will be devoted to the one and despise the other. You cannot." (Matthew 6:24)

"If you lend money to any of my people with you who is poor, you shall not be like a moneylender to him, and you shall not exact interest from him." (Exodus 22:25)

Reviews of the Author, Dan Jason (Financial Mentor)

"Dan is not only extremely knowledgeable at all aspects of finance, but he is also very graceful in his approach to how he teaches lessons. He doesn't single people out. He doesn't make students feel a certain way if they're really far in debt, or don't have the best income. Instead, he offers great advice and smart suggestions when someone comes to him with a question. He gives examples of how he applied what we're currently learning to his own financial situation while he was achieving financial success. The lessons that we learned, will stick with us for the rest of our lives, and it wouldn't have been possible without the dedication and knowledge of our teacher, Dan Jason." -John Y., student & advisee

"The resources he has, the knowledge he has, the fact that it's all based on his lived experience of the program and his own financial journey. It was also helpful to have Dan go through our budgets with us and discuss our financial situation. I liked the discussions when we could speak freely and go one on one about our situation or plan." -Sarah from New Orleans

"The best quality about Dan as an instructor was how down to earth he was about the whole course. He told his personal stories and related to us in ways we could understand and follow along. He was more of a friend than an instructor, we could talk to him side by side about anything. He was always willing to answer questions, look at our budgets and help us in any way he could. You know how you approach your mid 20's how you feel lost and confused about everything in the financial world? This class taught me more than I've ever known about that topic and I feel confident going forward knowing what the right decisions are to make. This class changed everything about the way I think of Money!" -Chloe A., mother & model

"This class did so much good for not only me but everyone in my life as I shared so much of what I learned with the people around me. I never thought I would understand some of the topics discussed, now I actually feel confident in what I am putting away for retirement. This class is amazing and the best practices for life!" -Carla T.

"My wife and I have learned so much in this class. Thank you for blessing our lives. You are a great teacher." -Bill O., age 85.

Money is a necessity that you cannot escape and we all need it to survive in society. Unfortunately, it is one of the lead causes for divorce, anxiety, stress, and unhappiness. Cash is king and capital can be your ticket to reaching your goals, achieving your dreams, and living the life you have always wanted. The best part is that you have the ability to start today with every choice that you make in order to set yourself up for a successful life. Whether you have been living in the trenches for some time now or you are staying afloat at the moment, today is the day that you can change some things that will radically improve your quality of life. Finances are not easy and debt is at times all consuming. However, the freedom that is available to you when you take complete ownership over your money is tremendous. Every one of us needs money daily. The easy solution is making more. Not quite. Certainly, having more capital can help, but it does nothing for us if we are not good stewards of our wealth. My hope is that you will decide to say "enough is enough" and put your foot down when it comes to your finances. Come along with me on a journey and learn the ins and outs of the financial world. Apply important and proven strategies. Start telling your money where to go. Through discipline, hard work, and change you will be able to pave your way toward financial freedom. By taking complete ownership over your finances, you will gain increased peace of mind and expand your net worth so you no longer struggle. The future is bright and the money is more green indeed on the other side. Learn how to take the baby steps towards financial freedom and gain key knowledge that will change your future and the scope of your family for generations to come!

www.ingramcontent.com/pod-product-compliance
Lightning Source LLC
Chambersburg PA
CBHW060412220526

45465CB00008B/2859